CONTAINMENT OR LIBERATION?

CONTAINMENT

or

LIBERATION?

AN INQUIRY INTO THE AIMS OF
UNITED STATES FOREIGN POLICY

James Burnham

NEW YORK

———————————————————

THE JOHN DAY COMPANY

Logicians have but ill defined
As rational, the human kind;
Reason, they say, belongs to man,
But let them prove it if they can.

Jonathan Swift

Acknowledgments

I WISH TO THANK the following for permission to quote from books which they have published: the University of Chicago Press, publishers of *American Diplomacy 1900-1950,* by George F. Kennan, and the Council on Foreign Relations, publishers of *Foreign Affairs,* in which the material from Mr. Kennan first appeared; Doubleday & Co., publishers of *A Foreign Policy for Americans,* by Robert A. Taft; Harcourt, Brace & Co., publishers of *America's Strategy in World Politics,* by George Nicholas Spykman; Harper & Bros., publishers of *The Future of American Politics,* by Samuel Lubell.

I also want to thank my wife for much help, including the technical preparation of the manuscript. I would dedicate this book to her, except that she is waiting for a very different kind.

Contents

Part One

CONTAINMENT

CHAPTER ONE

The Policy of Containment

FOR THE PAST SEVERAL YEARS the United States has had a foreign policy. This statement might seem to be as self-evident and therefore trivial as to say of a living man that he has been breathing. But it is not so. Heretofore in its history, the United States has had a foreign policy only in time of open war. Then, except in the case of the Korean War, there has always been a policy, direct and unadorned: to win a military victory. At other times there has ordinarily been no foreign policy at all.

The absence of a foreign policy did not mean that there was no discernible direction to the course which the United States followed through world affairs. A ship adrift on the open sea does not move at random. Under the orderly influence of current, tide and wind she progresses from one place to another. A distant observer might deduce that she was controlled by an eccentric navigator who was following a crude but legible chart. Because the current that has carried the United States is broad, powerful and uninterrupted, it is not always easy to distinguish destiny from design.

In the past Americans have been preoccupied by their own domestic development. No national election has ever been decided on an issue of foreign affairs. A war, even if it has long been rumbling on the horizon, has always caught the United States without an army. Foreign problems have been allowed to arise as if out of darkness, unforeseen and unprepared for. James Forrestal's journals record that the question of the disposition of the Japanese Emperor was not even discussed in any official circle until less than a month before the Japanese surrender.

Since 1947 the United States has had a foreign policy, a deliberate policy consciously elaborated, with theoretical underpinnings and a perspective into the future. This policy has not had the same degree of consciousness, rigor and dialectical showiness as, say, Soviet or pre-War Japanese policy. In their political behavior Americans are the least ideological of men. They are too "pragmatic" to submit all their actions to the master mould of a *Tanaka Memorial,* a *Mein Kampf* or a *Problems of Leninism.* At the same time, they have broken too sharply with tradition, and have too little sense of the past, to exhibit the empirical consistency of the British. Granted all these qualifications, a United States foreign policy has existed during these late years in a measure sufficient to arrange according to a discernible pattern nearly all important moves in foreign affairs.

14

Until 1947 the United States government was not mechanically equipped to determine and pursue a coherent foreign policy, even if its leaders had felt the need for one. Concern with foreign affairs was scattered among a variety of separate offices: Army, Navy, the State Department, the White House, the Treasury and still other agencies. Each worked largely on its own, with conflicting procedures and ideas. Except for Cabinet meetings where Departments not concerned with foreign affairs were also represented, and where foreign issues could seldom receive lengthy attention, there was not even a common meeting place for their chiefs. Apart from the President, who had much else with which to occupy himself, no one was charged with seeing that all those involved in foreign affairs should work in harmony toward the same objectives. Even within the Department of State there was no office or committee or even individual assigned to the task of surveying foreign policy as a whole. In accordance with the 19th century fetish of the division of labor, the Department of State was broken up into a myriad quasi-independent "area" and a few "functional" divisions.

The birth of a conscious foreign policy in 1947-48 was correlated with several changes in the organization of the government. There was first the unification of the military services in a Department of Defense, under a single Secretary of Defense on the civilian side, and a single military committee—the Joint Chiefs of Staff. This unification, though not complete in practice, lessens disputes between the military branches or at least provides an easier means for solving them, promotes unity in strategic planning, and "politicalizes" the military establishment in such a way as to bring it closer to the Department of State and the White House.

The second change was still more directly related to the development of a unified and conscious foreign policy. This was the establishment by statute of the National Security Council. This consists of the President, the Vice-President, the Secretaries of State, Treasury and Defense, the Chairman of the National Security and Resources Board, and (in an advisory capacity) the Director of the Central Intelligence Agency. In theory, it is charged with final determination and decision concerning all questions of national security and defense. The Council's membership, which groups together the chiefs of the agencies primarily concerned with the various phases of national security, reflects the statutory purpose. The Council does not yet have behind it the precedents and tradition that could transform its formal authority into practice. Up to the present it has not functioned as an autonomous body. It has rather been a conference of the separate members, each of whom continues to speak from the standpoint of his own separate agency. On the whole, the Secretary of State has been the dominating influence.

In spite of its deficiencies, the National Security Council does provide a meeting ground and a means of communication such as did not formerly exist. It makes possible a shift in bureaucratic terminology that might become in the future of the Council or of a successor-agency the symbol of a transformation in the American way of handling foreign affairs. Heretofore, a decision on foreign affairs usually took the form of a statement, paper or memorandum issued by the Department of State over the signature of the Secretary of State or one of his officers. Because the Department of State is formally in charge of foreign affairs as a whole, such a decision so issued is supposed to be a declaration of the entire government, binding on all agencies. In actuality, foreign policy decisions in modern times are not narrowly diplomatic, but have military, financial, commercial, "intelligence" and other consequences. A Department of State decision might not recommend itself to the differently placed interests of the Treasury Department or the military services. Since the chiefs of the Treasury and military regard themselves as occupying a governmental level equal to that of the Secretary of State, they are prepared to disregard a decision which rests formally on his authority alone. The only way out of the resultant confusions, by no means infrequent in American history, has been through intervention of the President in his official capacity. This solution was resorted to by Franklin Roosevelt, who thereby became "his own foreign minister," partly by taste perhaps as well as by necessity. It is an awkward vio-

17

lation of correct administrative practice, suited if at any time only for a grave emergency.

Since 1948, important decisions concerning foreign policy and national defense can take and more and more have taken the form of an "NSC directive." In that form, they are (in theory) superior to any individual Department, agency or office, including the Departments and agencies represented in the National Security Council itself. It is no longer the Department of State giving orders to the military, or the Treasury to either, but all agencies of the government receiving an order from a superior instance.

Prior to the establishment of the National Security Council, there was no organ of the United States government through which an integrated foreign policy could express itself, even if a policy had existed as an idea in someone's mind. The presence of the Council does not guarantee that there will be a policy, which requires individual brains as well as official committees. If there is one, the Council furnishes for its use a tongue and voice— a voice still much muted, inasmuch as NSC directives are normally Top Secret or higher in their security classification, but one loud enough to be heard in the relevant official ears.

At the same time that the steps were being taken to unify the military establishment and to institute the National Security Council, the Department of State made a parallel change in its own internal organization. The Department decided to establish a "Policy Planning Staff." According to its organizer and first director, "this staff was the first regular office of the Department of State to be charged in our time with looking at problems from the standpoint of the totality of American national interest, as distinct from a single portion of it. People working in this institutional framework soon became conscious of the lack of any general agreement, both within and without our government, on the basic concepts underlying the conduct of the external relations of the United States." *

Ambassador Kennan doubtless puts the problem backwards. It was not the creation of the Policy Planning Staff (or the National Security Council) that disclosed "the lack of any general agreement . . . on the basic concepts underlying the conduct of the external relations of the United States," the lack, that is to say, of a foreign policy. It was more probably the absence of an agreed policy in the context of a world situation which demanded one that prompted the establishment of these agencies.

It was fitting that the first chief of the Policy Planning Staff should have been the one to formulate the first foreign policy in the new mode. Since 1947 the policy systematized by George Kennan has been the working foreign policy of the United States.

Let us see just what this policy is. We can then try to

* George F. Kennan, *American Diplomacy 1900-1950*, Chicago, 1951, P. *v*. My subsequent quotations from Ambassador Kennan will also be from this book.

judge whether it is any good. It is no doubt an advance to have some sort of policy rather than none. But if the advance is in the wrong direction, the wanderer may be farther than ever from home.

2

The foreign policy pursued by the United States since 1947 has a recognized name: *the policy of containment*. This policy, which was gradually built up by many persons working in many different fields, has been expressed in hundreds of articles, speeches and declarations, especially those emerging from the Department of State. It was given systematic formulation by George Kennan, in his article, "The Sources of Soviet Conduct," published originally over the pseudonym "X" in the July 1947 issue of the magazine, *Foreign Affairs*.* Kennan expanded his thesis in a second article, "America and the Russian Future," which was published in the April 1951 issue of *Foreign Affairs*.**

The policy of containment as thus authoritatively stated by Kennan may be analyzed into the following elements:

(1) In "the mental world of the Soviet leaders, as well as in the character of their ideology . . . tremendous emphasis has been placed on the original communist thesis

---

* This article is republished in Part II of Kennan's book, *American Diplomacy 1900-1950*. It should be recalled that Kennan was chief of the Policy Planning Staff when he wrote the article.
** Also republished in Part II of Kennan's book.

of a basic antagonism between the capitalist and Socialist worlds." The "concept" "of innate antagonism between capitalism and Socialism . . . has become imbedded in foundations of Soviet power." The disturbing consequences for the Kremlin's conduct of foreign affairs "are there to stay, for the foreseeable future." *

Fortunately, "it is clear, from many indications, that this emphasis on basic antagonism is not founded in reality."

(2) The Soviet "concept" and its consequences mean "that we are going to continue for a long time to find the Russians difficult to deal with." Still, there is no immediate danger for the United States. "It does not mean that they should be considered as embarked upon a do-or-die program to overthrow our society by a given date. The theory of the inevitability of the eventual fall of capitalism has the fortunate connotation that there is no hurry about it. The forces of progress can take their time. . . ."

(3) "In these circumstances it is clear that the main element of any United States policy toward the Soviet Union must be that of a long-term, patient but firm and vigilant containment of Russian expansive tendencies." Moreover, "it will be clearly seen that the Soviet pressure against the free institutions of the Western world is something that can be contained by the adroit and vigilant application of counter-force at a series of constantly shifting geo-

* The quotations throughout this section are from one or the other of Kennan's two articles which have just been referred to.

21

graphical and political points, corresponding to the shifts and maneuvers of Soviet policy. . . ." This "policy of firm containment" is "designed to confront the Russians with unalterable counter-force at every point where they show signs of encroaching upon the interests of a peaceful and stable world." Secretary Acheson later expressed this last notion as "building situations of strength" in the free world.

The quotations in the above paragraph summarize the practical content of the policy of containment. We must now raise the problem of what the policy is supposed to accomplish. Must firm containment of "Russian expansive tendencies" go on forever? Or will the day some time come when we can sit back again, and relax? We find that Kennan permits himself an optimism that is something of a logical surprise after his description of the Soviet "concept."

(4) "Suppose that the Western world finds the strength and resourcefulness to contain Soviet power over a period of ten to fifteen years. What does that spell for Russia itself?" Happily, it spells a favorable change of heart in Russia's rulers. "The United States has it in its power . . . to force upon the Kremlin a far greater degree of moderation and circumspection than it has had to observe in recent years, and in this way to promote tendencies which must eventually find their outlet in either the break-up or the gradual mellowing of Soviet power." "A wise and adroit foreign policy . . . can serve to convince

the masters of the Kremlin that their grand design is a futile and unachievable one, persistence in which promises no solution of their own predicaments and dilemmas." If the masters should prove to be backward pupils in learning what is good for them, then "the institutions of the police state" will "sooner or later end up . . . by boring everybody, including those who practice them."

(5) By what mechanisms will this devoutly to be wished for consummation be brought about? What besides boredom is going to convince the masters of the Kremlin of their own stupidity, and gradually mellow the Soviet power? Here I am afraid that we have a little trouble getting a flat answer from Kennan's text. But the problem is hardly avoidable, and we find him frequently circling round it.

"How those changes are to come about is something which cannot be foreseen . . . With respect to the future of government in Russia, we see 'as through a glass, darkly,'" he reflects on page 151. After this appeal to the Bible, he turns to the mystical tradition of the Farther East: "If it should turn out to be the will of fate that freedom should come to Russia by erosion from despotism rather than by the violent upthrust of liberty, let us be able to say that our policy was such as to favor it, and that we did not hamper it by preconception or impatience or despair." If such is the will of fate, it is difficult to see why any policy at all, favorable or hampering, is required on our part.

Fate here is evidently in accord with basic "human nature," and the dictatorship "must" evaporate because it is evil and anti-human. "There can be no genuine stability in any system which is based on the evil and weakness in man's nature. . . . The day must come—soon or late, and whether by gradual process or otherwise—when that terrible system of power . . . will be distinguishable no longer as a living reality, but only as something surviving partly in recorded history and partly in the sediment of constructive, organic change . . ."

The prospect is even more hopeful than this rather timeless outlook might suggest. "Who can say with assurance that the strong light still cast by the Kremlin on the dissatisfied peoples of the Western world is not the powerful afterglow of a constellation which is in actuality on the wane? . . . The possibility remains (and in the opinion of this writer it is a strong one) that Soviet power . . . bears within it the seeds of its own decay, and that the sprouting of these seeds is well advanced." With the meticulous prudence of the trained diplomat, Ambassador Kennan adds: "This cannot be proved. And it cannot be disproved."

Kennan finally manages to carry his metaphysics down to one specific item: "the uncertainty involved in the transfer of power from one individual or group of individuals to others . . . outstandingly the problem of the personal position of Stalin," may affect the outcome. Even here his temperamental caution does not desert him: "It

24

is always possible that another transfer of preeminent power may take place quietly. . . . But again, it is possible that the questions involved may . . . shake Soviet power to its foundations."

(6) Is there any way that the United States, while meanwhile firmly containing, can aid the process of changing the hearts of, or in, the Kremlin? Evidently not much can be done, inasmuch as "of one thing we may be sure: no great and enduring change in the spirit and practice of government in Russia will ever come about primarily through foreign inspiration or advice. To be genuine, to be enduring and to be worth the hopeful welcome of other peoples such a change would have to flow from the initiatives and efforts of the Russians themselves."

Something may yet be possible, and "the most important influence that the United States can bring to bear upon internal developments in Russia will continue to be the influence of example." A united, happy, prosperous and peaceful America will convince the Russians, from the Kremlin down, of the error of their ways. The function—and the sole function—of the Voice of America is to make this admirable example known to the Russians, "to reflect as faithfully as possible the atmosphere and attitude of this country, in order that the Soviet citizen may form a fair judgment of them." For the Voice to slip over into political warfare would be a grievous error. Its function of reflecting "is an entirely different thing from urgings toward this or that political action. It would be a mistake" to suggest to the Russian "what he should do in the internal political life of his own country." We should stick to showing him "the form of the existence elsewhere on this planet of a civilization which is decent, hopeful and purposeful."

(7) The persuasive power of the example will be increased to the extent that the United States (and the free world generally) sets its house in order. The United States must "create among the peoples of the world . . . the impression of a country . . . which is coping successfully with the problems of its internal life and . . . which has a spiritual vitality. . . . It is a question of the spirit and purpose of American national life itself."

3

From these seven elements or principles of the policy of containment there follow a number of corollaries which bear on the practical application of the policy.

A. Though the international situation is rather bad, there is no emergency, and consequently no great rush. There is no reason to fear general war in the discernible future. No one need get panicky. Matters can safely be left in the hands of foreign service officers of the type of George Kennan and his colleagues.

B. In order to back up containment moves with a certain show of strength, and to prepare against the possibility of a general war in the distant future, the United States and its friends must rearm. Here also there is no hurry. We don't have to upset the American public or touchy allied statesmen with a drastic shift from butter to guns.

C. The policy of containment commits the United States to try to stop Soviet military forces from advancing beyond the territorial limits which they had reached in 1947. This seems unequivocal enough. Unfortunately, the policy is not equally clear about just those modes of warfare which are typical of communism. It does not indicate what to do when a thrust is carried out not by Soviet military forces in their own name but by non-Soviet communist formations or by nationalist, labor or other groups who may be under unadmitted Soviet control. Furthermore, it does not explain how to counter a communist advance that proceeds by political rather than territorial stages. What, if anything, follows from the policy of containment if the local communists of a given country, without any formal Soviet intervention, lead a general strike or a sabotage campaign, take over the trade union movement, enter or even get control of the local government?

D. The policy of containment excludes and prohibits offensive moves on the part of the United States which would carry across the boundaries of the Soviet sphere as these were established *de facto* in 1947. If such moves should be made, they would be contrary to and inconsistent with the policy of containment.

E. The policy of containment is incompatible with the conduct of serious political warfare. I propose to discuss the reasons for this in a later chapter. I have already referred to the fact that Kennan rejects political warfare as a method for dealing with "the Russians." In testimony before the Senate Subcommittee on Internal Security, Professor David N. Rowe stated that Kennan had in private conversation insisted that the United States could not carry on political warfare: "That is impossible. We can't do that kind of thing." *

F. From two points of view, the policy of containment dictates a program of international economic aid and rehabilitation. On the one hand, economic improvement is presumed to promote those conditions of strength that can resist both Soviet advance and communist infiltration. On the other, economic prosperity and progress are supposed to constitute the example which will persuade "the masters of the Kremlin" to desert the errors of their way.

---

* *Hearings* on the Institute of Pacific Relations, Part II, p. 3990.

CHAPTER TWO

Critique of Containment

THE POLICY OF CONTAINMENT was in accord with the liberal sentiment that has been prevalent in official American circles. At the time of its formulation in 1947, it was a natural enough response to the given world situation.

For many years Americans had been drugged by the social workers, fellow travelers and Soviet agents who penetrated the public opinion industry, and assembled in Washington under the careless scepter of Franklin Roosevelt. During the War they had been taught to honor and love Red Army commanders, Stakhanovite workers, "heroes of the Resistance," Soviet democracy and Uncle Joe. It was a shock when at the close of the war they saw their great Soviet ally gobbling one nation after another, with an appetite that seemed to wax only the greater by feasting. They observed that the Soviet union, unlike the other belligerents, was keeping its soldiers mobilized and its economy directed toward armament, not bathrooms. Some began to suspect that the Bolshevik leaders were taking their own program seriously.

With Eastern Europe, the Middle East and the Far East under Soviet attack, Americans began to realize that the security of Western Europe and of the United States itself was threatened. Fearing that Moscow might soon take over so much of the world as to make Soviet victory inevitable, Americans and their friends decided that they would have to mount some sort of counter-action. They neither wanted total war nor felt ready to fight one. They therefore tried to improvise ways short of all-out fighting to halt the Soviet avalanche.

This attitude and effort are the content of the policy of containment.

Nicholas Spykman, the late geopolitical theorist, wrote that "in the United States the word 'power' has a connotation of evil." The resulting "distrust of the moral character of power" complicates the problem of democratic statesmen, especially since the Industrial Revolution and the replacement of mercenary with mass conscript armies. The armed citizenry "needed a great deal more psychological training to overcome its natural preference for defensive action. . . . A conscript army does not fight for pay but for a national purpose, and unless public opinion is educated to the strategic advantages of offensive action or inspired by a messianic ideology, the nation will offer the lives of its sons only for national defense. To the man in the street, national defense means defense against attack, and attack is identified with invasion. To the general public the logical place to stop invasion is at the border, and border defense is the form of warfare which it intuitively prefers. This attitude satisfies two contradictory psychological needs of the good citizen, the requirement that he refrain from aggression and the requirement that he display virility in the defense of his home." *

The policy of containment might be called the Eastern college graduate's version of this instinctive viewpoint of the man in the street. Patriotism toward one's own country is out of fashion in the older Universities, so that the borders which the policy of containment worries about are those not of the nation but of that somewhat vague entity, "the free world." The rhetoric changes from the sturdy old Fourth of July phrases to the abstract, bloodless style of international conferences and official memoranda. But at its more polite and wordy level the theory of containment is a teacup edition of the ordinary citizen's normal bias, and similarly answers the two contradictory psychological needs to which Spykman refers.

Containment doesn't "threaten" anyone, not even the big bully loose on the block. It doesn't ask anyone to give up what he's already got. There is not a trace of "imperialism," "aggression," "preventive war," "the offensive," or any of those words that are taboo to liberal lips. White knight containment will merely stand up for the internationalist's version of hearth and home: collective security, peace, legitimate rights and the United Nations.

* Nicholas John Spykman, *America's Strategy in World Politics,* pp. 11 & 27.

Not only does the policy of containment thus recommend itself to the moral sense of many good citizens. It stirs more subtly another set of emotions less likely to be put on public display. Containment promises to solve the Soviet problem without any real sacrifice on our part. True enough, containment costs a lot of money, but money is the least of sacrifices, especially if spending it seems to be good for both business and politics. An armament program slow enough so that it doesn't interfere with civilian luxuries, but sufficient to be profitable and job-creating; international economic moves that put all the non-Soviet world inside our economic orbit; plenty of stimulating world travel for temporary and professional bureaucrats. . . . By a political slip, a few boys have been getting killed on a distant peninsula—a small price to pay for the sake of making televised speeches at the United Nations.

2

Though the policy of containment is attractive and natural, it is also wrong. In the remainder of this chapter I shall analyze its errors from the point of view of general strategic and historical knowledge. In chapter III I shall examine the actual record of containment in practice.

(1) The policy of containment is internally inconsistent. It both denies and presupposes the "coexistence of socialism and capitalism," as it is termed in communist propaganda.

32

According to George Kennan's argument, the Soviet government is in the grip of men who are unalterably committed to the belief that the continued coexistence of the Soviet union and non-communist nations is impossible. "Tremendous emphasis has been placed on the original Communist thesis of a basic antagonism between the capitalist and Socialist worlds. . . . This fiction has been canonized in Soviet philosophy . . . and it is now anchored in the Soviet structure of thought by bonds far greater than those of mere ideology." * It is in fact this doctrine that created the trouble that led to the policy of containment. The second half of the policy, dropping overboard this entire line of reasoning, blandly assumes that the "innate antagonism" will evaporate and coexistence become not merely possible but pleasing to the unalterably committed communist leaders.

Beneath the surface of a contradiction there usually lurks a consistent but vague point. I rather believe that what Kennan and the other State Department spokesmen of containment want is to communicate the following message to the Kremlin: You people often announce that you believe in the peaceful coexistence of capitalism and socialism. But you have been acting in an antagonistic way that endangers our vital interests. On our side, we believe 100% in peaceful coexistence, and we have certainly leaned over backwards to prove it. We can't help trying

---

* George Kennan, *op. cit.*, pp. 111, 113, 114.

33

to stop you when you threaten our security, but we are ready to go a long, long way to prove our sincere wish to be friends. Let's get together and really coexist.

This interpretation is in keeping with Kennan's press statement on the day in 1952 when he sailed away to take his post at the Moscow Embassy.

(2) From a strategic point of view, the policy of containment is purely defensive. It is defensive not merely through the omission of any offensive plan. The idea of containment deliberately excludes the offensive. If a Soviet force moves outside the 1947 boundaries of the Soviet sphere, then, theoretically at least, the policy of containment requires a *riposte*. It neither requires nor permits any action to be taken inside the Soviet sphere by an anti-Soviet force.

No lesson from historical experience would seem to be more thoroughly proved than the conclusion that a purely defensive strategy cannot succeed. "An absolute defense," according to Von Clausewitz, "completely contradicts the conception of war," and consequently of political struggle, of which war is a part. A defensive tactic at a particular point or moment, or a temporary strategic defensive, may be justified. A defensive tactic can indeed be an element in a strategic offensive. A defensive strategy can cover a necessary period for development or preparation, and can sometimes induce an unwary enemy to commit mistakes. But the defensive strategy must always be part of a larger plan that is conceived offensively, and that

34

waits for the decisive moment at which to seize the initiative and to launch the offensive campaign that victory always demands.

These lessons are as true in competitive business or sport as in war or world politics. A boxer may adopt a plan that keeps him on the defensive for a half dozen rounds. He will do so because he believes that thereafter he will be in better condition than at round one to carry the fight to his opponent. In order to win, he must do more than block blows. He must also hit.

"The lessons of history," Nicholas Spykman notes with ironic underphrasing, "throw serious doubt on the wisdom of the instinctive answer of the good man regarding the way to conduct a war. Strategy teaches that there can be no victory without offensive action, that mere defense of a border can bring a stalemate but no decision." *

As a temporary expedient, there was something to be said for containment. In 1946-7 the United States and its friends were not politically, morally or intellectually prepared to undertake a positive strategy against Soviet power. Some of them were in virtual collapse from the blows of the war, and the rest were in the middle of headlong demobilization. A defensive maneuver that while covering a shift in the cycle could perhaps slow the opponent's advance was in order, and about all that could be hoped for. The trouble is that the State Department

* *Op. cit.*, p. 29.

35

has insisted on transforming a temporary expedient into a principle.

(3) A defensive strategy, inadequate in every case, is triply so when applied to the Soviet Union. An opponent located in a relatively small territory, with a relatively small population, relatively weak in resources or passive in attitude, might be successfully "contained" for some while. On all counts, the Soviet Union is the opposite of such a convenient opponent. The Soviet territory is vast in expanse and perimeter. With the Soviet power holding the interior position, the borders cannot be sufficiently guarded from the outside. The population is 800 million; the resources, ample and varied. As for the Soviet attitude: not since the early days of Islam has a power drive been so dynamic.

Even these insuperable facts do not fully enough express the absurdity of the idea of defensively containing the Soviet power. It is absurd enough to suppose that anyone could contain an enemy with a border of more than 25,000 miles, but to restrict the Soviet border to 25,000 miles is a cartographer's deception. In the most profound sense there is no Soviet border. The Soviet power—that is, the power of its leaders to move men— extends by means of the world communist apparatus and the communist ideology into every nation and every community. To try to contain it is as futile as to try to stop a lawn from getting wet by mopping up each drop from a

36

rotating sprinkler. The truth in both instances is that to stop the flow we must get at the source.

Why possibly should we expect to contain the 800 million man Soviet Empire when we have not been able in five years to contain 10,000 communist guerillas in Malaya?

(4) The positive content of the policy of containment is the proposal to "build situations of strength": that is, to improve the economic, social and military condition of the non-communist nations so that they will become bulwarks against Soviet advance instead of victims prime for slaughter. The difficulty with this praiseworthy aim is that, under the perspective of containment, it is impossible.

Non-communist nations with large internal communist movements—like France, Italy, India, Guatemala, Indonesia, or Iran—cannot be developed into adequate containers of Soviet power because the communists will not permit it. The communists have both the will and the power to prevent it, and they will therefore do so in the future as they have in the past.

The situations of strength plan was drawn up as if the weakness of the non-communist nations resulted from "natural" causes: the damage from war and occupation; social backwardness (as in Asia); failure to adopt progressive forms of economic organization; inflationary or foreign exchange crises. Correct these by ample material aid, and the weakness would disappear. The plan took no

37

account of the fact that independently of such causes the weakness was also the result of the deliberate action of the communist enterprise and the Soviet state.

The communists conduct a double-pronged action against the non-communist nations. From within, the communist apparatus together with its dependent layers of fellow travelers, front organizations, dupes and innocents, corrodes the internal structure of the nation by propaganda, infiltration and subversion. From without, the Soviet state applies a dizzying mixture of pressure and cajolement, promises and threats, and at the same time secretly feeds and directs the internal subversive apparatus.

A program for strengthening the non-communist nations cannot be complete, therefore, unless it includes a double counteroffensive, designed to smash the internal communist movements and to set back the Soviet state. Because the Soviet Union is the central focus of the entire infection, the two objectives are necessarily linked. Containment, rejecting such a counteroffensive, can do no more than treat symptoms. The salve of dollar aid is applied to secondary irritations while the focus is left untouched.

So long as a large internal communist movement exists within a nation, a situation of anti-Soviet strength is unattainable. Organized communist movements neither wither nor fade away. They must be smashed. For this indispensable preliminary to strength, the policy of containment provides neither motive nor method.

(5) Even if containment could work, the result would be neither useful nor desirable. Let us imagine what successful containment would mean. Soviet power would cease its advance into new territory. It would remain at the borders of what would be recognized and accepted as the Soviet sphere. In 1947, when the policy of containment was formulated, that sphere was taken to include not only the pre-1939 Soviet Union but also the nations of Lithuania, Latvia, Esthonia, Poland, East Germany, Czechoslovakia, Hungary, Rumania, Bulgaria, Albania, the Soviet zone of Austria, Mongolia, Sinkiang, the Kuriles, and North Korea. Since then Manchuria, China and Tibet have entered the Soviet sphere, and have thus become subject to the policy of containment.

The policy of containment excludes the initiation of any action within the Soviet sphere. This exclusion means that the Soviet leadership is given a free hand to complete the consolidation of the newly conquered regions, and to promote their economic, social and political integration into the Soviet system. Politically speaking, containment can be interpreted in no other way by either the Kremlin or its subjects.

If the United States and its allies are serious about containment, they are saying to the Soviet leadership: move into a new territory outside the recognized boundaries of your sphere—into Greece or South Korea or West Berlin

39

or Western Austria, for example—and we will resist, even by arms if necessary. Stay at home to cultivate your posted acres, and we will not interfere in any way. Do what you want with the Poles, Czechs, Rumanians, Balts, Slovaks, Bulgarians, Hungarians, Albanians, Chinese, Mongolians, and with Russians, Ukrainians, Kazakhs, Chechens, Georgians and the others. Incorporate the satellite states juridically into the Soviet Union. Fill your slave labor camps. Perpetrate your genocides. Organize the industry and manpower of your great sphere into a colossal war-making machine. Establish a death zone at your borders. Replace Christian Europeans along your Western boundaries by collectivized Mongolians from the Siberian tundras. Russify the ancient cultures of Rumania, the Ukraine, Poland, Lithuania, Bohemia. Do all these things freely and without apprehension. So long as you keep the Red Army on your side of the line, we will neither interfere nor intervene.

This is the strict implication of the policy of containment. I will forego here any moral judgment, and merely observe that such an outlook is very far from meeting the requirements of elementary national defense, either for the United States or for its allies. The development and integration of the present Soviet sphere as a strategic unit would in itself be intolerable from a security standpoint. How could a man sleep secure if he lives in the path of a rock big enough to crush his house to bits, and poised to drop at the shove of a surly neighbor?

Looked at economically, the containment prospect is intolerable. If they are to slow the strategic buildup of the Soviet sphere, the non-communist nations must maintain a virtual economic boycott—which the Iron Curtain makes almost inevitable in any case. But over a long period such a boycott is economically close to impossible. It submits many of the non-communist nations to a strain much more severe than it imposes on the Soviet Empire. Western Europe cannot reach economic health, much less prosperity, without economic access to Eastern Europe and to China. For emergency and war purposes the strain can be endured, but the indefinite perspective of a world divided economically into two exclusive halves is economic insanity. Strict containment would be equivalent to the slow economic strangulation of the United States' principal allies.

(6) Whatever the differences over how it ought to be done, everyone will grant that the task of solving the Soviet problem will be long and arduous. Success will demand a heavy expenditure of resources, talents and courage. This demand cannot be met on the inert material level alone. Spirit must direct matter toward a goal, and a firm resolution must sustain an unyielding effort through periods of failure, loss and sorrow.

It is perhaps the crucial defect of the policy of containment that it is incapable of meeting this moral and spiritual demand. Who will willingly suffer, sacrifice and die for containment? The very notion is ridiculous. The

41

average man cannot even understand the policy of containment, much less become willing to die for it. Will the captives of the Kremlin risk death for a policy that starts by abandoning them to the usurpers of their freedom? Will the citizens of the western nations die willingly for the sake of running all over the earth to put out fires started by a gang of arsonists who are declared in advance to be immune in their own persons? They will die for their own flag, but how much will they choose to suffer for the flag of a "United Nations" which has been watered not by the blood of their ancestors but only by the words of international bureaucrats? How much will they sacrifice willingly in order to build situations of dubious strength in outlandish regions about which they know little and care less?

For a man to endure resolutely, he must believe that he is pursuing a goal—he must believe so even if the goal is in reality an illusion or a lie. The strange truth is that the policy of containment has no goal: it is a seeming paradox, a policy without a goal. If its defenders disagree with that description, then let them name the goal.

What is the goal, specifically, concretely? Is it agreement with the Kremlin? They will hardly say so. Their own analysis informs them such agreement is impossible, and that they will justifiedly be called appeasers if they make agreement the goal. Is the goal then the overthrow of the Kremlin, of the Soviet regime? Hardly, for that would negate the very "concept," as Kennan would call it, of containment. What is it then?

The policy of containment, stripped bare, is simply the bureaucratic verbalization of a policy of drift. Its inner law is: let history do it. We haven't got the intelligence, courage and determination to grapple with the Soviet problem head on. Let's duck the responsibility, then, and slip the ball to old mother history. Maybe she will do our work for us. To quote Kennan directly once more: "Who can say with assurance . . . This cannot be proved. And it cannot be disproved. But the possibility remains . . ."

3

The basic error of the policy of containment, underlying all of these specific errors which I have listed, is its failure to comprehend the revolutionary nature of the communist enterprise.

Though George Kennan is widely acquainted with the facts of contemporary history and has read an unusual amount for an active member of a government Department, he, like his colleagues, thinks in the categories of conventional diplomacy. He tries to bring the application of these categories up to date, and thereby shows his comparative superiority among Western diplomats and statesmen. He has not grasped the necessity for changing certain of the categories themselves. He knows by now that the Soviet state is hostile, and that this hostility is not a casual episode; and therefore he has notably advanced beyond the salad Harry Hopkins days. He does not yet realize that with the Bolshevik Revolution in Russia modern history shifted gears.

The policy of containment conceives of the Soviet Union as a national state in the traditional post-Renaissance sense: powerful, expansionist, dangerous, but nevertheless not differing in kind from the many other powerful national states of the past several centuries. This national Soviet state is conceived to have a government which, though curiously organized, is established and "legitimate," able to speak authentically for "the nation." Toward such a government, any of a number of standard political attitudes are possible. We might seek to establish a relation of friendship or alliance or neutrality or mere mutual respect and non-interference; or, granted other political indications, we might consider the relation to be one of friction, hostility, or war.

Since 1947 the political attitude of the Moscow government has seemed even to the conventional observer to be one of hostility, and its intention expansive. The traditional response is to try to erect an immediate barrier against the expansion, while constructing a balance of power unfavorable to the hostile and expanding government. If this power balance is attained, then the hostile government (Moscow) will be confronted with a choice between alternatives both of which give the advantage to the active opponent (Washington): either Moscow will continue hostility and in the end fight on a power basis weighted against her; or, accepting the new power relations, she will have to change her attitude, negotiate positively, and agree to some sort of *modus vivendi*.

Looked at in this way, the policy of containment is an example of classic balance of power politics. That this is the way in which Kennan and his associates understand it is made apparent by their semantic habits. Kennan, for example, uses the terms "Soviet Union" and "Russia" as if interchangeable. Such looseness would be of no significance in a routine journalist. In one who writes as a historian and political analyst, it reveals a basic assumption, and confusion, of major scientific importance. Even in relation to the pre-Revolutionary period, the careless use of the term "Russia" conceals the distinction between "ethnic Russia" (the nation of Russians which developed from the medieval Duchy of Muscovy) and the Czarist-ruled "Russian Empire," which included as many non-Russians as Russians, and dozens of non-Russian nations. Today the term "Soviet Union" carries a third meaning: the headquarters and central base of the world communist enterprise. Kennan's verbal usage shows that in his mind all three of these meanings are indiscriminately lumped together.

Kennan hardly ever refers to the world communist movement, seldom even to Russian communism. He discusses briefly, at an abstract and superficial level, a few items of communist ideology, but only, he explains, to get light on the nature of "the Russian rulers." He shows no acquaintance with or interest in the nature, structure and history of the communist apparatus and parties. His analysis is made and presented in terms of the behavior, history and prospects of national governments.

This mode of understanding is not peculiar to George Kennan. It is shared by all "official" thinkers on these matters, in particular by almost all persons who actively deal with such affairs in the Department of State and in the various American intelligence services. (In this respect, the Foreign Offices and intelligence services of the other major Western nations do not differ from the American.) Even the organization of the Department of State and the intelligence agencies expresses the underlying conception. The division of work and of administrative control is based on a system of "national desks." The critical information on what is happening in the world is supposed to be given to the leaders of the United States by a "national estimates" staff at the top of the Central Intelligence Agency.

If we want to find out what is happening in the world and what will happen, and to guide our own actions by that knowledge, we naturally cannot neglect the study of the behavior of national governments. For some problems of foreign relations such study is sufficient. The world power structure of the 20th century, however, is no longer exclusively organized in terms of the system of national states. New political forces, based on quite different—often non-territorial—principles, have intruded and erupted, with little regard for conventional boundaries or governments. These new forces are often the primary determinants of what happens.

Even in connection with France or Italy or India today, for example, it is an error to suppose that the governments are the authentic political spokesmen of unified nations in the sense that would apply to the French or British governments of 1860, say, or even the German government of 1880. Within the boundaries of France, Italy and India, substantial percentages of the population do not recognize the official national governments as in any sense "their government." These dissidents ("separatists," General De Gaulle calls them) belong in reality to dual or opposition "Nations," the local seats of which are not official buildings but clandestine rooms that transmit orders from "desks" in Bucharest, Peiping or Moscow.

The error is at its maximum in the case of the Soviet Union. It is true that in one perspective the Soviet Union can be understood as a nation in the traditional sense, with a national government which sits in the Kremlin. This is how Kennan and his colleagues understand it. From this point of view, the Soviet state is simply a new form of the imperial Russian government of pre-1917, subject to the same pressures and impulses that have been operative throughout Russian history.

In another perspective, which has remained up to now outside of the range of Kennan and his colleagues, the

Soviet Union is not a nation, state or government in any conventional meaning, but the main base of an unprecedented enterprise which fuses the characteristics of a secular religion, a new kind of army, and a world conspiracy. The idea of "containing" a particular nation which comprises a definite population enclosed by definite territorial boundaries is certainly not absurd, even though it may be impossible in a given instance. It is hard to see even what it means to try to "contain" a universalistic, militant, secular religion, based on a vast land mass inhabited by 800 million humans, which has irrevocably set itself the objective of monolithic world domination, and which already exists and acts inside every nation throughout the world.

On the "national" interpretation, it also makes some sense to hope as Kennan did that, if containment succeeds, agreement with the Soviet national government may some day become possible. Comparable shifts in governmental attitudes, bowing to political realities, have often occurred in the past. If we view communism as religion and conspiracy, we find that it excludes in advance any possibility of agreement with *the infidel,* and utilizes the mechanism of negotiation only as one more weapon in the struggle for total power.

When Ambassador Kennan left for Moscow at the beginning of 1952, he stated that he was going to his new post with the hope that he would be able to lessen existing tensions, remove misunderstandings, and promote a new attitude on the part of the "Russian" government which would lead to negotiation and agreement. There is no reason to believe that his declaration was mere diplomatic double-talk. His stated purpose was in accord with the policy of containment, in which he believes. It was realistic and attainable in terms of the theoretical presuppositions of the policy of containment. Stalin, who does not share those presuppositions, was evidently a dull pupil to the scholarly envoy. Before the end of the first year, Kennan was thrown out.

CHAPTER THREE

Containment's Record

IN 1947 THE POLICY OF CONTAINMENT became the established foreign policy of the United States government.

The first important act of the containment period was the decision to support Turkey and Greece in their resistance to communist pressure, which in the case of Greece was taking the direct form of armed rebellion. This decision was embodied in a message sent by President Truman to Congress in March 1947. By May 1947 Congress had passed a bill authorizing the assistance to Turkey and Greece, and appropriating the initial funds.

It is noteworthy that except for the decision to fight in Korea this curtain raiser was bolder than the acts that have followed. There are, indeed, some analysts who consider the policy of containment to be a retreat from "the Truman Doctrine" that was applied to Greece. However, the intervention in Greece was undoubtedly in accord with the principles of containment as these were afterwards formulated. The non-communist Greek government was under armed attack by a communist force. The

50

Greek communists were notoriously subject to Moscow's command, and thus an expansion of Soviet power. Truman proposed to "contain" the Soviet power at the borders of the recognized Soviet sphere.

The Greek intervention accepted also the negative principle of containment: that there should be no anti-Soviet initiative, and that no counter-action should be carried across the border. During the subsequent Greek fighting, we had as a consequence the first sample of the communist "protected sanctuary," of the type which has become familiar in connection with Korea, Indochina and northeast India.

On June 5, 1947, General George Marshall, then Secretary of State, spoke at the Harvard University Commencement exercises. There he made the first public statement of what came to be called "the Marshall Plan," a principal element of the over-all containment policy. Situations of strength were to be built in the free world by massive infusions of economic and technical aid. The United States government, Marshall said, will help European governments that are "willing to assist in the task of recovery." Disavowing any American assumption of the strategic initiative, Marshall went on: "Our policy is directed not against any country or doctrine but against hunger, poverty, desperation, and chaos. Its purpose should be the revival of a working economy in the world so as to permit the emergence of political and social conditions in which free institutions can exist."

Public Law # 472, signed April 3, 1948, brought together in one document most of the elements of the policy of containment. The junction is charted by the four Titles of this law: I, "The Economic Cooperation Act of 1948"; II, "International Children's Emergency Fund Assistance Act"; III, "Greek-Turkish Assistance Act of 1948"; IV, "China Aid Act of 1948." The preamble described Law # 472 as an Act "to promote world peace and the general welfare, national interest, and foreign policy of the United States through economic, financial, and other measures necessary to the maintenance of conditions abroad in which free institutions may survive and consistent with the maintenance of the strength and stability of the United States." President Truman, on signing this Law, called it "America's answer to the challenge facing the free world."

A kind of ideology of containment took form. This has been consistently expressed in the issues of the digest, *United States Policy toward the USSR and International Communism,* which show to what a surprising degree the policy of containment has functioned as a "general line."

In March 1952, President Truman reviewed the doctrine in a message to Congress: "We are joined with other countries in the patient and systematic building in the free world of enough military strength to deter external communist aggression; and of economic and political and moral strength to remove internal threats of communist

subversion and point the way toward democratic progress." A few days later, Secretary of State Dean Acheson
continued before a Congressional Committee: "The
American people have clearly rejected both isolationism
and preventive war * as self-defeating courses of action.
. . . What the Mutual Security Program represents is our
share of the total effort which is now going on, to reduce
the weakness which stands as a temptation to aggression,
and to build instead a strong and confident structure of
peace. . . ."

In May 1952, the State Department published an article by Charles B. Marshall, a member of the Policy Planning Staff. The original principles of containment, as
crystallized over five years, were restated. "Coexistence
with the Soviet Union," Mr. Marshall somewhat disin-
genuously insisted, "is not simply possible; it is a fact."
He explained, in the State Department dialect, that U. S.
policy works along three general lines:

> The first is to make coexistence more tolerable. . . .
> The second line is to prevent serious deteriorations
> in the conditions of coexistence by avoiding losses in
> areas of sharp political conflict.
> The third general line relates to the development
> of international usages and institutions of responsi-
> bility as instruments of free collaboration among na-

* "Preventive war" is the term used by the spokesmen of the Department
of State to refer to proposals that the United States should attempt to recover
the strategic initiative.

tions instead of the collaboration by intimidation offered by the adversary.

In an address delivered that same month, Francis H. Russell, Director of the State Department's Office of Public Affairs, answered the question, "What is our basic strategy, our blueprint for victory?" His reply is identical in substance with Kennan's articles of 1947 and 1951. It includes: (1) the rejection of the initiative; (2) the reliance on automatic "natural" influences for softening the communist tyranny; and (3) the perspective of a future day when negotiation and agreement with the Kremlin will become possible:

> It [our basic strategy and blueprint for victory] is that we maintain and, where necessary, increase the free world's strength . . . on the assumption that, confronted with this strength . . . the police state will suffer from its inherent weaknesses, the master plan of the Kremlin will perforce and in time fall apart, and will be replaced by something more amenable to the decencies of international life.

This, then, has been the policy. Let us now review what has actually been done under the policy, and from the results strike a balance.

2

Two consequences of the policy of containment are indisputable. Many committees have been formed, and much money spent.

The policy of containment has been carried on in part by agencies which predate its adoption but which have become integrated into its program. The principal American administrative instruments which have been newly created for containment's sake are the Economic Cooperation Agency (ECA) (now deceased), the Mutual Security Agency (MSA), and the Technical Cooperation Agency ("Point 4"). In connection with these and with the North Atlantic Treaty Organization (NATO), innumerable international agencies, committees, boards, staffs, etc. have sprung up. The United States has also attempted to bring into line with containment the United Nations and its subsidiary agencies, for all of which the United States is the chief financial contributor: the International Bank for Reconstruction and Development, the International Monetary Fund, the Food and Agriculture Organization (FAO), the World Health Organization (WHO), the Economic and Social Council (ECOSOC), and the United Nations Educational and Scientific Council (UNESCO). The Export-Import Bank has been frequently brought in. The stepped up propaganda and information activities of the Department of State as well as the expanded armament, mobilization and redeployment program are also part of the containment activity.

Because of the dispersion of the program over so wide a field, and because many of the activities (including considerable rearmament) would have been carried out under some other motivation even if the policy of containment had not been adopted, it is impossible to determine exactly how much containment has cost. A few rough figures will give some notion of the financial order of magnitude.

Non-military aid granted by the United States to foreign nations under ECA from that agency's birth in 1948 until its formal expiration on December 30, 1951, came to $11 billion. Under the ECA provisions, and subject in its use to ECA control, each recipient nation had to set aside a "counterpart fund" in local currency equal to the amount received in U.S. aid. The ECA international total can therefore be considered double the 11 billion in dollars.

Post-war loans from the United States, including some made before 1947 but excluding those by international agencies such as the International Bank for Reconstruction and Development, totalled through 1952 approximately another $11 billion. Aid to Greece and Turkey came to about $700 million. Money allocated to what was officially called "Civilian Relief (Occupied Countries)," in effect equivalent to Marshall Plan aid for Germany and Japan, reached through 1952 the remarkably high figure of $6 billion. Even the Philippine Rehabilitation program cost more than $600 million. Military aid to foreign nations has been rising steadily, and is expected to total about $6 billion in the fiscal year ending June 30, 1953. The general military budget is not publicly broken down so as to show just how much has been spent from it on the occupation of Germany and Japan, aid to Indochina, and fighting in Korea, but the sum is high in the billions.

The policy of containment has developed through two principal phases. In the first, which lasted from the beginning (1947) until the latter part of 1951, the emphasis was on economic rehabilitation. The sums spent for foreign economic aid exceeded, at first very heavily, those spent for military aid. In the second phase, which after overlapping the first replaced it at the end of 1951, the ratio has been reversed and the emphasis put on military assistance.

In the economic field, the most significant new departure during the containment period has been a half-step toward West European economic integration. In 1950, Robert Schuman, the French Foreign Minister, proposed a scheme, known popularly as "the Schuman plan," for pooling West European steel and coal production under an international authority. This plan, strongly favored by the United States, has slowly made some headway.

On the military side, the principal development has been the formation of the North Atlantic Treaty Organization (NATO). NATO began with the signature of the

Atlantic Treaty in April 1949, and by 1952 included the United States, Canada, Greece, Turkey, and all of the nations of Western Europe except Switzerland, Spain and Sweden. (In 1952 Western Germany was brought into NATO, but with a special status.) Through NATO the military strengthening of the West, in particular of Western Europe, is supposed to be carried out. NATO's structure consists of a rapidly expanding series of "councils," "committees," "headquarters," "staffs," and so on. Various contingents of the respective national armies are placed at the disposition of NATO's "Supreme Headquarters Allied Powers Europe" (SHAPE). NATO's most novel military feature is the plan for a one-uniform "European Army" made up of units from France, West Germany, Italy, Belgium, the Netherlands and Luxembourg, and subject, according to the organizational chart, to a hierarchy that starts with a political Council, and descends through an Assembly, Commissariat and Court to a Central General Staff, various lesser staffs, and ultimately, it is hoped, to troops.

The American part of the containment is not, of course, confined to foreign economic and military aid. Internally, the post-war demobilization was halted and reversed. Though the pace of rearmament, in keeping with the relaxed containment outlook, has remained sober, its scope was soon sufficiently large to absorb considerably more money than the total of all forms of foreign assistance.

Along with rearmament, the United States has expanded its program of information, propaganda, and "psychological warfare." This is in accord with the principles of containment, which call for such a program on two grounds: to give moral support in the labor of building situations of strength against communist advance; and to acquaint "the Russians" with the admirable "example" that is going to lead them to the path of international virtue. Though this information program is based primarily on radio, it includes also many kinds of publicity, cultural exchange, advertising, posters, books and pamphlets, movies, libraries, lectures, subsidies, leaflets, public relations and scholarships, carried out not only through the Department of State but by many official, semi-official and private agencies.

In reviewing the content of the containment program we should not forget that there has also been a good deal of fighting. This has been widely distributed: in Burma, Indochina, Malaya, Greece, Indonesia, the Philippines, Iran, Tunisia, Egypt, China, Korea, Tibet, and small but unpleasant skirmishes in a number of other places such as Nepal, Berlin, India, Guatemala, and the air space above the Baltic. Many men of many nations have been shooting and dying in these fights. Billions of dollars worth of American equipment and hundreds of thousands of American men have been used in them.

3

Because certain omissions also follow logically and unavoidably from the policy of containment, we must add to this summary of what was done a note on some things that were not done.

During this entire containment period no attempt has been made to push Soviet power back from the western line which it had reached in 1947, or from the eastern line which it attained in 1950 by the completion of the conquest of the Chinese mainland. No offensive anti-Soviet action has been taken. No initiative that would reach into the Soviet sphere has been tried or sought. There has been resistance to Soviet initiative, on some occasions and in some places. There has been defense against communist offensives, and counter-action to Soviet originated action. But the exclusive commitment to the defensive has been maintained.

We have noted that this exclusion of the offensive is a strict deduction from the theory of containment. Therein may be found the explanation for some notable events since 1947 that are otherwise so puzzling that critics of the State Department have inclined to attribute them to faulty intelligence, official stupidity, or even personal treachery in high places. Such factors have not been altogether absent, but in determining what has and has not happened they have had less importance than the reigning policy.

Consider, for example, the city of Berlin. There the boundary of the Soviet sphere is plainly drawn for everyone to see, along the center of well known streets. The communists operating from their sector of Berlin have retained the uninterrupted initiative, and have carried out one offensive action after another against the Western sectors. They blockade the Western sectors; buzz and shoot up planes approaching them; raid houses and shoot or kidnap scores of individual citizens; send their gangs roaming through the streets; order tens of thousands of young people to parade provocatively; enclose villages, houses and fields that they suddenly decide belong inside their territory. The Western powers protest in vehement letters and memoranda; they spend hundred of millions of dollars to carry food and fuel through the blockades; they tighten police work in order to discourage the kidnappings and to keep the streets from being altogether at the mercy of the Eastern gangs. In short, they try to "contain." But never an incursion under their prompting into the Soviet sector; never a disputed village taken over by a patrol from the West; never a nuzzle to a Soviet plane; no anti-communist youth marching through the streets of East Berlin; and never—God and Acheson forbid!—the kidnapping of a sturdy communist. In the "protected sanctuary" behind the magic line of the sector boundary, every communist, like a Brunnhilde behind a wall of fire that even Siegfried has sworn to respect, can sleep secure.

Greece was not different in principle. With supplies

and orders and men from Moscow, the guerilla bands fought in the north, and raided into the valleys of the interior and south. Helped by American equipment and officers, the Greek army fought well. Time after time the guerilla forces were defeated in battle only to be saved from annihilation by retreat across the borders of the Soviet sphere. Back in their sanctuary they could regroup, and receive the supplies, guns and training without which their ranks would have shriveled. No plane or patrol or shell from the free world sought them out.

Nor is it changed in Korea. There we have been so tender of the good Soviet name that we have not even named the aggressor. We fight against the shadow of a shadow—the Korean satellite of the Chinese satellite of the central sun. At the Yalu, the planes of the free world come up against the barrier of containment, a barrier demonstrably harder to pierce than Stalin's curtain of iron. On the ground, the armistice line is drawn along the thirty-eighth parallel, decided by the principles not of fighting but of containment. That parallel was the boundary of 1947 and therefore sacred.

Wherever a weak spot appears in the non-communist world—in Tunisia, say, or India or Indochina or South America—Moscow is left free by the policy of containment to exploit it to the feasible limit. If the weakness exists or appears inside the Soviet sphere—in Albania or East Germany or Soviet Turkestan—all western eyes turn discreetly aside as gentlemen from a lady immodestly exposed by the snapping of a strap or window shade. Woe to the western statesman or soldier so imprudent as to suggest that some of the Soviet weaknesses ought to be boldly probed or even grappled! The wrath of the State Department, Containment's strict defender, will come thundering about his ears. If he is an American he will soon find himself in the doghouse of enforced retirement.*

"We will not be provoked!" declare the administrators of containment. And they have made good their boast, in small things as in large. No plane shot down, no use of diplomatic immunity for spying and subversion, no citizens kidnapped, tortured or imprisoned, no vile accusation of the lowest crimes, no months long captivity of a consul or a soldier, has moved the State Department one hair's breadth from the even tenor of containment's way. The containers seem resolved to give the Kremlin a heroic proof that friendly coexistence will always and permanently be available for the asking.

4

The objectives of the policy of containment may be listed as the following: containment itself, in the literal territorial sense; containment in the more general sense of holding back any extension of Soviet or communist

* *Cf.* the fate of Major General Orville Anderson, founder of the Air War College; Lieut. General Albert Wedemeyer; General of the Army Douglas MacArthur; Stuart Symington, first Secretary of the Air Force.

power; building situations of strength in the sense of improving socio-economic conditions; building military strength; the internal weakening of the Soviet Union; setting a good democratic example, and informing the world thereof. If we use these objectives as our standard of assessment, what are the net results of the containment program?

A. In Western Europe, the territorial line has been held.

Yugoslavia, still under communist control, has seceded from the Soviet sphere. Though this action represents a weakening of Soviet power and thus a relative improvement in the position of the non-communist world, it did not occur as a result of the policy of containment, and is therefore irrelevant to an assessment of the results of that policy.

From the territorial point of view, the great shift since 1947 has been in the Far East. There the policy of containment proved unable to hinder the extension of the Soviet sphere over the whole of mainland China and Tibet. A bitter struggle continues in the attempt to check further advance into South Korea and Southeast Asia.

B. There are several nations outside of the recognized Soviet sphere where Soviet-directed communist power, while not in control of the central government, is established within certain sub-territories and there exercises *de facto* sovereignty. From the point of view of containment, these situations are leaks in the dike which are capable of very rapid enlargement. They are analogous to "the Yenan way." In China, the communists managed to set up jurisdiction over a section of the country, at first relatively small. This section, under "the Yenan government," served first as a fulcrum for operating on the nation as a whole, and then when opportunity arose, as a base from which the rapid subjugation of the entire nation could be achieved.

These neo-Yenans exist conspicuously today in Southeast Asia—in Burma, Malaya, and Indochina. They exist also, at one or another stage of development, in India, Nepal, the Philippines, Indonesia, Guatemala, and perhaps in several of the Arab countries. In one or two of these cases the communist position may be weaker today than at containment's inauguration in 1947. In others, including the two—Indochina and India—which are strategically the most important in the present phase of the world struggle, the communist hold has hardened.

These Yenan situations offer a challenge to the policy of containment more direct than anything except an open advance by the Soviet army. The fact that they do exist and have in critical cases been aggravated since 1947 is a large minus quantity in the account book of containment.

C. The policy of containment has not succeeded in building any major "situation of (socio-economic) strength." Several South and Central American countries are in comparatively good shape, probably better than in 1947 and better than their normal. This cannot be attributed to the policy of containment, under which virtually nothing has been done for South and Central America.* Switzerland, Sweden, Norway, Denmark, Belgium, Ceylon, Australia, New Zealand are reasonably healthy. Switzerland and Sweden are outside the active containment scheme (neither is a member of NATO), and all of these small nations together do not weigh very much in the world balance. Canada is of course healthy and steadily stronger, but her population is still small, and in any case she must from a strategic and economic point of view be considered part of the United States.

The policy of containment was first of all oriented on the three major nations of free Europe: Britain, France and Italy. In spite of about $15 billion that have been poured into them since the war period ended, none of their principal economic, social, fiscal or moral problems has been solved, and several of their key difficulties have become more grave since 1947. The exchange crises recur, the franc still wavers, Italian unemployment and mass misery persist, Aneurin Bevan's anti-Americanism and pro-appeasement expand, the communist hold on the Continental trade unions is unbroken, the communist vote is maintained, England's austerity diet is unsweetened, neutralism flourishes, French housing continues to crumble.

* The prosperity of Uruguay, for example, is actually an expression of the failure of containment. It rests largely on the flight of nervous capital from Western Europe.

The newly independent nation of India has yearly famines, clasps hand with communist Peiping and flirts with Moscow, vents its economic frustrations in squabbles over Kashmir and metaphysical lectures to the world at large, and expresses the acuteness of its social crisis by communist successes in general elections. India, far from being a situation of strength helping to counter Soviet pressure, is a liability, one more drain on the available and not infinite resources.

Since 1947, pointed by events in Iran, Egypt, Tunisia and Morocco, there has been a severe decline of Western standing in the Arab world. Though this has not been solely the result of communist pressure, I am inclined to believe that hidden communist strategy has had more to do with it than is generally recognized. Whatever the exact cause of the Arab troubles, they deprive the non-communist world of needed assets and open up another breach to easy Soviet penetration. In the Arab world also, the policy of containment has not merely failed to build situations of positive strength but has not even contained.

The only major nations which since 1947 have noticeably increased their socio-economic strength are the defeated powers of the second World War, Germany and Japan. It will be a joke on History's part if the salvation of mankind from total Soviet conquest relies in the end on Germany and Japan. It will also be a melancholy indictment of the policy of unconditional surrender and national annihilation that was attempted toward them.

Fortunately perhaps, Japan and Germany were not annihilated, and the Pentagon seems to think that they may come in handy.

In spite of their considerable recovery, neither Japan nor Western Germany is yet a firm situation of anti-Soviet strength. Neither has a regular armed force or functioning armament industry, and these are not built in a day. Both operated until 1952 under the artificial Occupation economy, and are starting on their own deprived of many of the resources, people and spaces on which their pre-war strength had been organized. Both are subject externally and internally to a variety of tensions and conflicts. Neither is politically stable, and both need trade with what is now the Soviet sphere. Both, moreover, are painful allies for many of their former enemies.

D. Since 1947, the one marked increase in non-Soviet military strength has been in the case of the United States itself. Even at the relatively slow pace of rearmament, this increase has been formidable. The growing military might of the United States is a factor of the greatest world significance.

American military strength is not specifically an achievement of the policy of containment. The seriousness of the Soviet danger has been recognized for some years by nearly everyone in the United States, whether or not they agreed with the ideas of containment. No substantial group has opposed rearmament and remobilization. As a matter of fact, the pace of rearmament would have been faster under certain of the alternative policies.

Apart from the United States, the increase in the military strength of the non-communist nations has been minor. Available forces are probably readier for combat, but the actual expansion has been small. At the end of 1952, the Soviet-directed Polish army was larger than the army of any non-communist nation except the United States.

There has been a bit of fakery about NATO. On paper the NATO army is an impressive outfit, but it is a long way from tables of organization to troops in the field or planes ready for combat on an airstrip. The NATO notion seems to be that a fighting force can be built out of public relations. After every NATO conference, communiqués are issued to advise the world that new and greater goals were set, swarms of combat divisions and coveys of new air squadrons scheduled for the end of whatever year it is, and so on. After a few weeks it comes out that what chiefly happened was another round of squabbles over staff titles, disputes about the propriety of Germans, Spaniards and Turks dying for freedom, and the creation of a new layer of high echelon committees.

E. The policy of containment anticipates and predicts the progressive internal weakening of the Soviet system by the combined effect of its own evil nature and the free world's good example.

The Soviet Empire does have many weaknesses, but

judged relatively it is internally stronger, less weak, than
when containment began in 1947. The policy of containment has had in fact exactly the relation to Soviet internal development that follows logically from its principles.
Containment has granted the communist leadership an
undisturbed internal hand. Disregarding Kennan's ex-
hortation to repent of their dictatorial sins, the communists have not too unnaturally used their time to shore up
their walls.

An ideological purge and party reorganization have
eliminated many of the cracks which were sprung in the
party apparatus during and just after the war. Armament
industry has been enlarged, and reconstruction of war
damaged areas carried through without interference.
Atomic capability has apparently been achieved. The prestige of the leadership has been fortified by its demonstrated ability to keep the world initiative and by the
great victory in China.

By renouncing offensive action, containment abandons
the satellite (captive) nations to Moscow. This implication
of containment, which does not escape the Kremlin or the
peoples of the satellite nations, helps create a political
climate favorable to the consolidation of Moscow's control
over the satellites and their integration into the Soviet
system. Though this process is far from complete, there
are two rather ominous signs of Moscow's growing confidence. At the end of the war, Moscow shipped machines and factories from both East (Manchuria) and

West (Eastern Europe) into the Soviet interior. After 1950 this transfer was not only stopped but reversed. Especially in Manchuria, Poland, Czechslovakia and East Germany, a program of industrial expansion was set into motion. Along parallel lines, several of the satellite armies, reduced to nominal size immediately after the war, in 1950 began to build up again.

F. According to the policy of containment, the United States was to set a good example which would be communicated by radio and other media in a great "campaign of truth." Either the example or the communication seems to have been lacking. There is no real evidence that American propaganda is accomplishing much inside the Soviet sphere, except possibly in one or two of the satellites (in particular, Czechoslovakia and East Germany). As for the non-Soviet world, anti-Americanism is probably at a new height, and is certainly wider and sharper than in 1947.

Let one example be eloquent. In France, after more than $5 billion in grants since the war, not to speak of two rescues from military defeat in a generation, there is not a single newspaper or magazine with an editorial policy that is pro-American or even consistently friendly to America. This vacuum is really amazing. In France the United States apparently cannot even buy or bribe a paper to be friendly, though buying papers and editors is a custom not unheard of in that country.

This review of containment's record has been made in the light of containment's own objectives. The preceding chapter found reason to conclude that certain of the objectives of containment are incorrect, undesirable or impossible. Here we discover that even if we accept these objectives as legitimate the policy of containment has not in practice been able to advance them. They are, in fact, further away than when the attempt at containment started.

Political leaders who are in power always incline to the view that there is no use raking over the coals of the past. One may sympathize with this injunction if the poking into the past is only the maneuver of an opposition to tarnish a reputation or gain a cheap factional advantage. There are pasts and pasts, however. Some of them are dead, and should be thoroughly buried, to be exhumed only by disinterested historians under suitable scientific auspices. Other pasts, whether we like it or not, continue to live actively through the present and into the future. To review the record of containment is not to perform an autopsy but to diagnose the condition of a still breathing organism.

If the policy of containment is wrong, the error is large. What is at stake is quite literally our possessions, our freedom, and for very many of us our lives. And it is wrong. The evidence proves that it is wrong. Expressed in the crudest terms, we are just not getting enough for our time and money. Let me at once add that I do not criticize the amount of time and money that has been spent, though that amount is vast. We seek a prize that could hardly be cheap. The difficulty is not the money but the fact that we are not getting anything for it.

Because the policy of containment is wrong, and has been proved wrong by history and experience, it is time to change it.

Part Two

GEOPOLITICS

CHAPTER FOUR

The West European Strategy

FROM A GEOGRAPHICAL POINT OF VIEW, the policy of containment expresses itself as a West European strategy. When they are criticized for neglecting some other region of the world more favored by the critic, this is sometimes denied by the spokesmen for containment, who prefer to say that they pursue a "global strategy." In a sense this is true. What is going on is a world struggle that affects and is affected by events in all parts of the earth. Even so, it is not possible to be equally active everywhere at once. There must be one rather than another emphasis, some particular concentration of forces. In the program of containment, the emphasis and concentration are unquestionably on Western Europe.*

---

* Concerning a discussion which he had with George Kennan in 1949, Professor David Rowe testified as follows before the Senate Subcommittee on Internal Security:

"First, he said, 'China doesn't matter very much. It's not very important. It's never going to be powerful.' I attributed this kind of mistaken view to his complete history of involvement in European politics. He approached the Russian problem from the point of view of Europe. Mr. Kennan said once in my hearing some years before this time that the struggle between ourselves and the Soviet Union will be resolved somewhere on a line drawn between

The revealing symbols of the financial accounts do not leave this strategic fact in doubt. Under the policy of containment more than four-fifths of the international subsidies and credits from the United States have gone into Western Europe. Virtually nothing (less than one percent) has gone to South and Central America. Most of the small portion allocated to the Far East has been spent in connection with the occupation of Japan.

Though not quite so extreme, the military concentration has been the same as the financial. It seems clear that the unadulterated policy of containment called for no sizeable military forces in Asia except for the garrisons in Japan, the Philippines and Okinawa. Following the adoption of the policy of containment, American troops were withdrawn from Southern Korea, a move of what might be called containment in reverse. In China, American troops left in face of the advancing Red Army. There was no American force in Formosa, and it was shown in 1949 that the containers anticipated the transfer of the island to communist control.

The containment plan was, and is, that Western Europe should be the scene for the major and only serious military buildup, with the Far East given a minimum priority for a long time to come. This plan has been

Stettin on the north and Trieste on the south. I considered this an extremely limited view and I questioned him at the time about where the Far East came in the settlement of our problem with the Soviet Union, but never got any satisfactory answer out of him."

Hearings on the Institute of Pacific Relations, p. 3987.

dislocated by two events which were, from the point of view of containment, unforeseen accidents. One was the massive communist attack on Southern Korea. The second was the establishment of the Chinese Nationalist Government on Formosa with a solidity which the communists have not felt themselves able to crack. If foreign policy spun out its logic in a vacuum, even these two events might not have brought any deviation in containment's course. As it was, with pressures from internal public opinion, the felt needs of international anti-communist morale, and President Truman's temperament all brought to bear, consistency had to yield to fact. Without any alteration of basic policy, West European military concentration was lessened in order to send troops to fight in the East.

Within this West European perspective there are, of course, secondary disputes. Some of these concern strictly military problems of maneuver, equipment, prepared lines, bases, training and supply. Others involve the more fundamental question of how to forge Western Europe into a functioning politico-military entity. Shall the West European containment machine be built around Britain or France or West Germany? What role in West European security is to be given to the non-democracies, in particular to Spain and Yugoslavia? The continuing debate on such issues has presupposed the common strategic outlook.

2

From the standpoint of United States policy makers, there is a diverse motivation, not always consciously understood, for adopting a West European strategy.

In the first place, there is the basic cultural fact that the United States is an offshoot of Western, Christian civilization, the historical origin of which is in Western Europe. To cut off from Western Europe would be matricide, an act of cultural impiety, and would isolate the Americas in an alien cultural sea. It is a fine thing, certainly, when East and West drink their cocktails together in the United Nations' Lounges, but even with a million Eleanor Roosevelts, it will be a while yet before the sons of European civilization can be culturally as close to Hindus, Buddhists and Mohammedans as to each other.

Europe is part of America's destiny, of her fate. Even if European power were reduced much further than it already has been, it would not be possible for the United States to disregard Europe or even to assign Europe a tertiary role in American plans. If America has enough material strength to go it alone, her cultural and spiritual resources remain inadequate, and these are also necessary for survival. Alone, America could not maintain her historical existence against the overwhelming spiritual mass of an otherwise non-European, non-Christian world. If

Europe declines to defend herself, America will still have to defend her.

There is some reason to believe that what now appears as a world crisis is in historical substance the crisis of Western Civilization. On that hypothesis, what is at issue is the question whether Western Civilization can overcome its tendency to self-destruction, unify its own material and spiritual forces, and assume responsibility for constructing a workable world polity. Success could hardly be expected if the West began by cutting itself in half.

Economic and technological grounds can also be urged for a West European strategy. Western Europe possesses an advanced technology and an economic plant capable of turning out large quantities of strategically significant products. It has in particular the invaluable asset—a heritage that cannot be improvised—of many millions of highly trained workmen, technicians, scientists and professionals.

The West European and American economies, yoked together under the guidance of a common policy, decisively overweigh the economy of the Soviet sphere and of all the rest of the world. On the other hand, if the Soviet Empire should succeed in embracing the West European economy, it would be a close to insurmountable disaster. Western Europe, besides adding to the quantitative weight of the total Soviet potential, would supply qualitatively just what the Soviet economy most lacks and needs.

On the more directly military side, the demonstrations of the past do not permit us to dismiss Western Europe. If her armed forces are run down, they are even today not negligible. More important for the future, the West European nations have a tradition, a popular training, a social context and a skilled military nucleus (cadres) out of which it would seem that powerful fighting forces could be fairly quickly formed. The relation of the total social milieu to the problem of building a fighting force is often overlooked. To build a modern army, air force or navy is an exceedingly complex business. It can't be done out of central Africans in central Africa. The 300 million Moslems in the belt from Indonesia to Morocco, who are a favorite topic for strategic discussion, do not live in the kind of social and historical environment from which a modern armed force could be produced in a time short enough to bear on current strategic calculation. Western Europe does constitute such an environment. Militarily speaking, Western Europe seems to be a bird if not in hand at least in reach.

Reinforcing all of these factors which favor a West European strategy is the weight of psychological inertia. This is the way it has always been in the past. This was the strategy followed for the two great wars of the 20th century. If the total results of these wars were not altogether satisfactory, military victory was at any rate won in both of them. Even during the 19th century, when the intervention of the United States in world affairs was less active, it was Europe and the European balance of power that were the primary concern of American foreign policy. Orienting on Europe means walking the old familiar beat.

This natural inclination to stick in the groove is strengthened by personal pressures. Thousands of adroit, intelligent West Europeans make it their business to keep influential Americans favorably disposed toward their countries. Within the American political establishment there are many individuals whose education and taste link them to Western Europe.

With much of the motivation for a West European perspective one must agree. We are justified, I think, in concluding that a correct foreign policy for the United States will include the attempt to defend Western Europe. It does not follow that the defense of Western Europe is the sole or even the principal objective of a correct policy, nor does it follow that the best way to defend Western Europe is by the policy of containment and the military strategy associated with it. It may be that Western Europe will be best defended by directing the political focus of American policy elsewhere.

83

3

The West European strategy, adopted by the United States as the expression of the policy of containment, entails the effort to build a West European bloc. The old balance of power policy, pursued toward Europe by Britain and imitated in the past by the United States, always meant the effort to prevent European consolidation. Today Washington sees the European problem quite differently. Its aim is to discover or construct a balance to the weight of the Soviet Empire. For this purpose, Western Europe as a whole is little enough, and is quite useless if internally divided and self-neutralizing. Washington must therefore promote the consolidation of Western Europe.

This attempt, inescapable granted the policy, is pushed within the economic, military and political spheres. From its beginning, the Marshall Plan was handled on a regional as well as a national basis. Frequent conferences of all participating European nations were held. Allocations of funds were made in these plenary meetings. A European Payments Union was formed. Tariff reductions, customs simplification, interlocking of facilities such as railroads and power lines were advocated. The United States favored the special agreements linking the economies of Belgium, the Netherlands and Luxembourg (Benelux), and the Schuman Plan to place European steel and coal under supra-national direction.

Military consolidation has been carried further than

economic, at least on paper. Under the North Atlantic Treaty Organization, there are a permanent Council and a permanent Military Committee of the participating nations. The Supreme Headquarters with a supranational general staff is actually functioning, and plans are drawn for a European Army. The source of the chief pressure for consolidation is symbolized by the fact that Supreme Headquarters is under the command of an American.

On the more directly political field, the United States backs the various movements for European federalism or unity, and approves such manifestations of these movements as the Strasbourg "Council of Europe" and "European Assembly." These movements invariably speak of "Europe" without any qualifying adjective. In all cases, however, the concrete political meaning is "Western Europe." In speeches, interviews and articles, there is a certain amount of talk about Europe as a whole, especially from professional one-Europers like Paul-Henri Spaak, André Philip, Salvador de Madariaga, Henri Brugmans, Duncan Sandys, and their American admirers. But you can't change the objective meaning of a policy merely by talking.

In the present period, the effort at European consolidation is a derivative of the policy of containment. That policy seeks to prevent further Soviet expansion, but it excludes actions aimed inside the borders of the Soviet Empire. Eastern Europe lies inside those borders. It follows that the only part of Europe toward which containment permits positive action is Western Europe. That this limitation holds is continuously manifest in practice. In the "European" conferences, councils, committees and staffs, there are representatives only of the West European nations. There is the same restriction in the membership of the Strasbourg Assembly and Council of "Europe." All of the funds for "European" economic and military aid are allocated to Western, none to Eastern, Europe.

It will doubtless be argued that this could hardly be otherwise. The East European nations are at present part of the Soviet Empire, under the political control of Moscow. Including them in the American-backed European program (which would in any case not be permitted by Moscow) would be equivalent to helping the Soviet Empire instead of helping the non-communist world resist the Soviet Empire.

This persuasive argument itself shows the influence of the containment outlook. One who rejects containment might reply: It is not true that the East European nations are part of the Soviet Empire. The governments of these nations have been usurped by agents of Moscow's imperial tyranny, which for the moment holds the nations captive. In the case of some of them (the Baltic nations, Poland, Ukraine), free governments exist even today, though on foreign soil. For the others, there are national representatives more genuine than the men of Moscow. From a military point of view, are not Generals Anders and Bor-Komorowski more authentic leaders of the Polish nation than Moscow's Rokossovski? For all of these nations, there is also the future.

Why then should not all of the East European nations, through their free representatives, participate in the actions that aim at the strength and unity of Europe? Why should they not sit in the committees, conferences and staffs, and share in the aid and subsidies? Why should there not be Polish, Rumanian, Byelorussian, Czech, Ukrainian—and Russian units in the European armies, as unquestionably as French, West German or Italian? What European reason is there to exclude gallant and able East European officers from the Staff of SHAPE, the allegedly Supreme Headquarters Allied Powers Europe? In the European Movement and the Strasbourg institutions, which are primarily propagandistic and symbolic, what is the objection to giving East European representatives equality with those of the West? In all of these instances, it is not the undoubted practical difficulty but the effect of the policy of containment that explains the systematic omission.

Experience has disclosed that the program for West European consolidation, which follows from the policy of containment, is simultaneously a program for East European rejection. The moves which are designed to cement Western Europe into an economic, military and political unit attached to the United States also tend to push Eastern Europe toward the East, and to aid the consolidation of Eastern Europe as a counter-unit attached to Moscow.

87

In the language of political action, the program of containment tells East Europeans that the West has abandoned them and that Washington is ready to come to terms with Moscow on the basis of the 1947—or even the 1949 world division: that is, on the basis of the communist enslavement of Eastern Europe and China.

On a world scale, the West European concentration helps the Moscow propagandists to play up the idea that the present struggle is between "East and West." In terms of Europe, it is objectively true that containment transforms the struggle into a combat between East and West. From this fact as a starting point, the propagandists slide into the false but potent suggestion that "East versus West" means Asia versus Europe and the United States.

The Korean war is a confirmatory example of how the policy of containment favors the "East-West" demagogy. Apart from the Koreans themselves, the actual lineup on the battlefield has been on the whole East versus West. Containment does not permit the use of Chinese Nationalist troops, because that would be implicitly an offensive action directed against the Soviet sphere. Containment does not encourage the presence of other Asians and Africans, who have been represented only by a handful of Siamese and Turks. Under a different policy they might have joined in substantial numbers. Whether or not this would prove of much military help, the political difference would be immense.

4

The military perspective of the West European strategy seems to be a simple projection of the strategy that was followed during the first two World Wars. Planning for the second World War took over the strategy of the first, and merely added more emphasis on the new weapons— tanks and planes—that had begun to be felt in 1918. Planning for the third proceeds in much the same way, with the increased emphasis this time on strategic bombing, pilotless air missiles, and nuclear armament.

It is assumed that the Soviet Union will start the third World War with a massive attack, as Germany started the first two. The communist armies will pour west across the north European plain, and through the Balkan gaps. The North Atlantic armies will defend in a delaying action, and will strive to hold a small European bridgehead. North Atlantic sea power will keep supply lines open, and will prevent any Soviet thrust over water. Meanwhile, strategic bombing of Soviet centers will begin—though there is no clear decision as to just how and where this bombing will go on: whether as rapidly and heavily as possible, or drawn out; whether only on the Russian centers, or on the Russian plus non-Russian Soviet (*e.g.,* Ukrainian) centers, or also on the satellite centers and those captured by the Red Armies in Western Europe.

Then what? Presumably a war of attrition with a long, slow buildup. Then an enlargement of the bridgehead,

89

or the conquest of one if the entire Continent will have been lost, and the landing of mass armies on the Continent. Then the overland advance, beating the communist-led forces back mile after mile, to—it would seem —almost anywhere: Moscow, the Urals, Lake Baikal, Vladivostock, Magadan . . . ?

The North Atlantic armies will be faced with the forces of Eurasia. Behind the North Atlantic lines and inside the military units, the trained activists of the communist apparatus will be at the disposal of their Soviet masters.

Even granted that such a prospect is not militarily fantastic, the North Atlantic High Command faces two dilemmas that seem almost insoluble. The first concerns Germany (that is, West Germany). It is not possible to build an adequate force from Western Europe unless Germans are included. Reasoning from this premise, American policy has come to view German rearmament as the key to the entire European defense problem. But if Germans have a too conspicuous place in the North Atlantic forces, the jealousies and fears of other West European nations, especially France, will mar the cohesion of the North Atlantic bloc.

Much more grave is the possible result on the other side of the line. Balts, Poles, Czechs, Slovaks, Hungarians, Rumanians, Ukrainians and other East Europeans dislike the Russians, and hate the present Russian-dominated

Soviet government. But they also hate Germans and German governments. In some cases, their hatred of the Germans goes a long way back. In all, it is fed by the memory of German frightfulness during the second World War. The Russians also, whatever their attitude toward their present communist masters, fear and hate Germans. They too remember the Nazi terror, which in their minds is identified as German terror.

I do not think that the problem created by the anti-Germanism of Eastern Europe is altogether insoluble. I believe, however, that if German troops appear as principal forward elements of the North Atlantic armies, the political result will be to convince the East European units that what they confront is only a disguise for the second World War all over again. Their anti-Germanism will tend to cancel their anti-communism, and to consolidate them behind Moscow.

I have already mentioned a second dilemma in which the West European strategy is caught. Within France and Italy there are mass communist movements built in layers around a core of trained activists. In other West European nations communist influence is considerable. A European defense force must draw a large portion of its units from these infiltrated nations, especially from France and Italy. But we may affirm it as a law of contemporary social life that nations within which communism is a mass influence cannot have mass conscript armies able to stand up to communist armies.* The mass conscript armies, taken from the population as a whole, must inevitably include large numbers of communists and fellow travelers. These will bleed the armies from within, by sabotage, treachery and subversion. Apart from this direct effect on the armed force, the existence of the mass internal communist movement destroys the national morale that is needed to sustain a mass army.

The usual debate over the NATO armies revolves around questions of how many divisions will be ready when. What possible difference does it make how many divisions NATO has, if they won't fight? The West European strategy, under the dominion of the containment idea, fails to allow for the fact that the first requirement for the armed force which it seeks is not arms or planes or dozens of divisions but the will to resist and to fight. The presence of communism on a mass scale is both a cause and a symptom of the lack of that will. The perspective of containment is unable to call it forth.

The Soviet Empire is weaker and the United States potentially stronger than the general opinion allows. It is perhaps conceivable, therefore, that the war could be won through the West European strategy that is imposed by the policy of containment. If so, it is hard to see how victory could be made much more difficult and expensive.

---

* The French army in Indochina, which has fought well against communism in that difficult war, is not a mass conscript army, but composed in large measure of trained cadres and professionals. The majority in the ranks is in fact German.

5

Many Americans, becoming impatient with Europe, have begun to berate Europeans for laziness, corruption, cowardice, unwillingness to sacrifice, ingratitude, civic irresponsibility and sundry other vices. Particularly disturbing is the wide-spread European attitude of "neutralism," which holds that Europeans should be neutral as between the Soviet Union and the United States, both of which are in their respective ways equally imperialistic and barbarian. Before becoming too self-righteous about these European ailments, Americans should realize that they share responsibility for them. Specifically, neutralism is simply the European face of the Washington-minted coin of containment.

The running European complaints about American policy need not mislead us. Most Europeans are really quite content with the policy of containment, as they plainly show by the stands they take on internal American politics. And why should they not be?

Except for the communist minority, Europeans fear and dislike communism and the Soviet Union. They do not want their countries to become part of the Soviet Empire or their social system to undergo a totalitarian transformation. At the same time they do not feel that they have the power to resist the Soviet advance. The only source of a sufficient power is the United States. Therefore Western Europe welcomes American power as a counterweight to Soviet power. While the two great power centers balance each other, Western Europe occupies a more or less neutral ground between them, and is given a breathing space, a ground for a certain amount of maneuver. This ground is made more agreeable by the heavy flow of financial irrigation from one end of the balance.

Western Europe does not want to be conquered by the Soviet Union but it also does not want war. It does not feel able to fight a war, and judges that whatever the outcome, there would be a long if not a permanent stage of European occupation together with both physical and cultural destruction. Pressed by both fears—of conquest and of war—the best practical solution, as the average European sees it, is to have American power brought to bear just sufficiently to check further Soviet advance westward, but not strongly enough to risk actual war either through Moscow's coming to the conviction that it must start fighting before it is overwhelmed, or by Washington's being tempted to seek a "definitive solution."

This state of affairs preferred by most Europeans, is, it will be seen, identical with what is sought by the policy of containment. Therefore most Europeans support the policy of containment, are favorably disposed to the American spokesmen for containment, and attack the critics of containment. Many Europeans flavor their support with anti-American rhetoric. Except when this comes from communists, it should not be taken too literally.

The Europeans know that there is no future penalty for anti-Americanism, as there is for anti-Sovietism. Besides, it is always hard for a man to forgive someone whose help he needs.

I have frequently heard American officials ask what causes European neutralism and what might combat it. Unfortunately, they are not willing to listen to the true answer, namely, that their own policy, the policy of containment, is the principal active cause of European neutralism, and that the only way to combat it is to change to a positive, dynamic policy. Containment means that the United States and the Soviet Union are playing each other off. In the stalemate that is thus produced, Western Europe can maintain a precarious independence. If the dual world balance were broken in favor of the Soviet Union, then European liberty and civilization would be destroyed. If it were broken in the other direction, in favor of the United States, then Europe, if not quite so badly off as under Moscow, would lie at the mercy of the United States. Europeans are convinced, moreover, that a decisive outcome in either direction would involve general war.

Reasoning thus, Western Europe does not want a decisive outcome. Its governments therefore draw frantically back from any action on Washington's part that looks as if it might be moving from the defensive posture of containment toward the offensive. In every international kitchen, from Panmunjom to Berlin to SHAPE headquarters to the United Nations Assembly, the West European cooks rush to keep the political pots from reaching a boil.

The West Europeans cling to the indefinite stalement which the policy of containment serves to enforce and prolong. The remarkable paradox about the policy of containment is that under it the United States, spending and doing much more than under any previous foreign program, never leaves the starting place. In economic and political fundamentals, Western Europe remains just where it was in 1947. There are the same communist parties, the almost identical communist vote in elections, the same export and exchange crises, the same unemployment in Italy and absence of housing in France, the same diet in England, the same lack of significant military power, the same conferences and the same speeches.

Under containment, the effect of United States aid has often been to continue rather than to solve the problems of Western Europe. The mythical European "dollar gap" is a striking example. Apart from United States subsidies there neither is nor can be a dollar gap. If a European nation doesn't have dollars, then it can't make dollar purchases. No proposition in bookkeeping could be simpler than that one. Of course a nation may want to spend more dollars than are being earned by the unsubsidized workings of its own economy (and it may be desirable from an American standpoint that it should do so). The Marshall Plan provided West European nations with extra dollars. The only "dollar gap" is the difference between what the unsubsidized European economy could have purchased in dollars and what it did in fact purchase. This was exactly equal to the Marshall Plan subsidies, and will continue to be equal to whatever subsidy is allocated in the future.

Since it is the American subsidy that creates the dollar gap, we may be logically certain that no amount of subsidy, even if prolonged for a million years, will ever overcome the gap. What the indiscriminate and loosely administered subsidies have actually tended to do is to make it less urgent for the European nations themselves to undertake the internal reforms that might increase their dollar earning power or decrease their need for dollar purchases.

A similar analysis applies, at least in part, to the military field. Though it is true that Western Europe cannot defend itself by its own resources, it can do much more than it has done. But why should it? If the United States is ready to supply enough planes, bombs and men to stand off the Soviet Union, what is the reason for Europeans to strain themselves?

The point of view from which West Europeans welcome the containment-neutralism stalemate is in reality negative and short-term, and places them in an ambivalent condition. It is well and good that Moscow and Washington play each other off, and thus give Europe a little elbow room. But the stalemate also leaves Western

Europe frustrated socio-economically, deprived of any motive for effort and accomplishment. If Western Europe is to continue to exist, it has to have somewhere to go, something to do. It cannot stay shut up within the containment boundaries. To the East, the Iron Curtain blocks the greater part of Eurasia. The door is closed to one after another region of the Far and Middle East. The United States, dominating the two Americas, is strict with outsiders. The cost of the stalemate, of standing still, is so heavy that Europe does not have enough surplus left to begin the great task of the development of Africa.

The West European strategy based on the policy of containment is in the long run without hope. If Europe is finished in any case, then a feasible strategy cannot be based on Europe, and all money, arms and effort spent on such a strategy are wasted. If Europe still has a future, then it will be won only when Europe breaks out of the containment bottle, resumes an adult international responsibility, and once more carries on a world-significant work. To break out of containment means primarily to enter or reenter active relation with the vast portions of the earth now closed by Soviet power and intrigue. There are only two ways in which this can happen: either by capitulation to Moscow and absorption in the Soviet Empire; or by the ending of that Empire through the liberation of the lands and peoples now subject to Moscow's tyranny.

CHAPTER FIVE

The Asian-American Strategy

EXCEPT FOR THOSE whom they accuse of seeking "preventive war," the spokesmen for containment usually call their critics "isolationist." Since the critics seem thereby convicted of living hopelessly in the past, in total disregard of such manifest facts of the present century as two world wars, international fascism and international communism, this use of terms is good demagogy. It is doubtful, however, that many bona fide isolationists exist any longer, or have existed for some while back.

Isolationism used to mean the belief that the United States could be economically, politically and militarily self-sufficient within its own continental boundaries, that it had nothing to fear from any foreign foe, and that it had no need for overseas territories, alliances, interventions or entanglements. So early as the declaration of the Monroe Doctrine (1824) this strict isolationism enlarged its coverage from the actual United States boundaries to the limits of the Americas. By the time of the Spanish

War, nearly all Americans were ready to look still further, beyond one or the other sea.

A strong current of American opinion opposed entry into the first World War, and one almost as strong was against entry into the second. This anti-interventionist opinion, especially its midwestern section, is ordinarily called "isolationist." Recent empirical study seems to prove that the source of anti-interventionism, in the case of both wars, was not an isolationist or even a pacifist attitude, but ethnic sentiment. Samuel Lubell has reported the relevant findings:

> To some degree all Americans share the traits commonly associated with isolationism—a hatred of war, a suspicion of foreigners, dislike of militarism and a reluctance to have one's sons drafted. . . .
>
> What I found raises the question whether isolationism, as generally pictured, ever really existed. Possibly because it seemed to concentrate in the Midwest, the belief developed that isolationism grew out of the physical insularity of the American interior. Midwesterners were presumed to be less sensitive to events abroad than coastal residents and more likely to feel that the United States could live alone and get away with it.
>
> This concept of isolationism must be discarded. It is a myth. The hard core of isolationism in the United States has been ethnic and emotional, not geographical.

By far the strongest common characteristic of the isolationist-voting counties is the residence there of ethnic groups with a pro-German or anti-British bias. Far from being indifferent to Europe's wars, the evidence argues that the isolationists actually were over-sensitive to them.

This ethnic factor emerges even more strongly in World War Two.*

Lubell's analysis shows that we should always search for the concrete political position which under the given conditions may be expressing itself in an isolationist form.

2

There are several quite different points of view from which the prevailing policy of containment has been opposed. As yet, none of these has received an accepted name and organized formulation. Probably the most prominent has been the doctrine which the spokesmen for containment call "isolationism," and whose champions in turn characterize the containers as "interventionists" or "Eastern internationalists." This doctrine has been sharply expressed by the Chicago *Tribune,* and more moderately put by General Douglas MacArthur, Senator Robert Taft, and by other (though by no means all) Republican senators and congressmen. Whatever name may

* *The Future of American Politics,* by Samuel Lubell. Harper and Bros., 1952. Pp. 131-2.

be given to the policy that can be assembled from these various sources, I propose to call the geopolitical outlook which goes with it the "Asian-American strategy."

The Asian-American strategy rests on three geopolitical ideas, one negative and two positive.

The first idea is to decrease the emphasis on Western Europe that has characterized American foreign policy throughout this century and that is continued in the policy of containment. The extreme opponents of containment suggest, without quite saying so, that Western Europe should be allowed to go it alone, that economic subsidies should be stopped and United States ground troops withdrawn from European soil. A more moderate opinion grants that some aid to Europe is necessary, but that it should be much reduced from the containment level. Whatever the quantity of aid, Europe should not be the political and strategic focus. Senator Taft has written:

> Before the Russian threat, I was very dubious about the policy of advancing money to Europe in such large amounts [but] . . . the question today . . . is hardly an issue on which there is a serious split. . . . All of this aid has been extended to Western Europe out of all proportion to our aid to the rest of the world. . . .
>
> If these [European] nations really do desire to build up their own arms and if it appears that that defense has a reasonable chance of success I believe we should commit some limited number of American

divisions to work with them to show that we are not evading the toughest part of the defense program provided by the Atlantic Pact. Such a program, however, never ought to be a key point in our strictly American military strategy.*

The second premise of the Asian-American strategy is that the United States is itself the primary strategic base, and that the strengthening and immediate (local) defense of the United States are the tasks which should receive unquestioned priority. Again in Senator Taft's words:

> I do not believe it is a selfish goal for us to insist that the over-riding purpose of all American foreign policy should be the maintenance of the liberty and the peace of the people of the United States, so that they may achieve that intellectual and material improvement which is their genius. . . .
>
> Our first consideration must be the defense of America. . . . This country is the citadel of the free world. The defense of the United States itself is, of course, the first goal of our own people, essential to protect our liberty; but it is just as important to the rest of the world that this country be not destroyed, for its destruction would mean an end to liberty everywhere. . . .**

* Robert A. Taft, *A Foreign Policy for Americans*. Doubleday & Co., 1951. Pp. 85, 99.
** *Ibid.*, pp. 13, 14, 74-5.

This second idea has direct practical consequences. Those who believe it are always more critical than "internationalists" of proposals to export American money, arms or troops. They pay more attention to the possible internal economic effect of a given plan than to what it might be expected to accomplish—for good or ill—abroad. They tend to favor military measures which bear directly on home defense: troops stationed within continental boundaries; radar screens and anti-aircraft installations; lots of fighter planes at domestic bases.

The third idea is that greater strategic emphasis should be put on Asia, in particular on the Far East. "Broadly speaking," Senator Taft writes, "my quarrel is with those who wish to go all-out in Europe, even beyond our capacity, and who at the same time refuse to apply our general program and strategy to the Far East." *

The motive for favoring a more Asia-inclined perspective is no doubt often factional. Republicans believe that one of the major failures of recent Democratic Administrations has been in the field of Far Eastern policy. Not unnaturally, they have wished to exploit this failure for factional advantage. At the same time, there are also more impersonal considerations by which an increased emphasis on the Far East can be supported

It is argued that the policy of containment, with its West European strategy, seeks to lock the front door while leaving the back door open and unguarded. Even if

Ibid., p. 112.

Soviet power could be stopped for an indefinite period in Europe, the fate of the world can be decided meanwhile in Asia. Asia contains vast territories and the bulk of the world's population. If the communists succeed in organizing Asia's space and inhabitants into a going system, then they will have a more than adequate geopolitical base from which to achieve world domination. What will it benefit the United States to hold all of Western Europe if it thereby loses China, Southeast Asia and India?

Viewed more positively, America has many potential allies in the Far East. The religions and cultures of Asia are incompatible with communist ideology and counter to much of communist practice. The peoples of the Far East do not wish to escape from Western imperialisms only to become subject to the new imperialism of Moscow. If we prove that our interest is not limited to European white men and that we are ready to collaborate loyally with Asians, then we shall find—it is argued—that the Asian peoples will effectively resist communist encroachment.

3

Let us now review critically these three central ideas of the Asian-American strategy: less emphasis on Europe; first priority to the strengthening and local defense of the United States; greater relative emphasis on the Far East.

That the first and supreme concern is the central base (in which I would include Canada and the Caribbean basin along with the continental United States) seems to me entirely correct. I believe that the spokesmen for containment and the overly "internationalist-minded" in general—the world government enthusiasts, global humanitarians and all-out United Nationalists—are inclined to neglect this axiom of a proper United States strategy. Nations like individual men must put their first reliance on themselves. No matter how many "situations of strength" are built elsewhere, they will be of no use if in building them the situation of the United States becomes weaker.

If the liberty of the United States is to be defended and the Soviet goal of world domination blocked, the principal source of the requisite supplies and arms must inevitably be the economy of the United States and Canada. These two must also supply the hard and leading sector of the military force. There is no way in which the United States can get rid of its responsibility. If others were capable of assuming it, the present relations would be reversed. It would be the other nations that would be trying to build a situation of anti-Soviet strength in the United States, not the United States in them.

It does not follow that the integrity of the central base is most surely guaraneed by defensive and domestically concentrated strategy or tactics. This is the mistaken politico-military conclusion which isolationist sentiment draws from a partially correct premise. You don't always defend a city best by putting all of your troops behind its walls. It may be more effective to keep a force outside, ready to cut the enemy's communications, to fall on his rear or seize his home base. Nicholas Spykman rightly observes: "Most of the successful wars of history have been carried on in other peoples' territory." *

Military analysts have long recognized that successful defense of the United States is impossible from within its own national boundaries or even on a hemispheric extension. "The power potential of the Americas," Spykman affirms, is "inadequate to balance the Old World. . . . There is no safe defensive position on this side of the oceans. Hemisphere defense is no defense at all." **

This conclusion suggests that the factories of Detroit might be better protected by planes stationed at a base in, say, Pakistan, than by many squadrons operating from the Detroit area's own Selfridge Field.

The defenders of the Asian-American strategy are correct when they reason that Soviet conquest, consolidation and development of the Asiatic Coastlands (China, Southeast Asia, India) would make eventual Soviet world victory certain. This threat from Soviet success in the Far East is, however, comparatively long-run, not immediate. Neither China nor Southeast Asia nor India can for many decades reach a technological and economic level that would permit them to become autonomous war-mak-

* *America's Strategy in World Politics*, p. 27.
** *Ibid.*, p. 457.

ing powers in contemporary style. So far as offensive capability against America goes, they can at present serve only as adjuncts to and in some respects drains on Soviet military power. For the short term, Soviet consolidation of Western Europe would be, as the spokesmen for containment argue, a greater danger to the United States than Soviet conquest of all Asia.

This relative ranking of Europe and Asia has always been recognized by the communists. They adopted their own Asian strategy as admittedly a second best. Contrary to the expectations of orthodox Marxism, the communist world revolution had begun not in one of the highly industrialized nations, but in backward Russia. The leadership was aware that the revolution had to be either extended or defeated. Granted the geopolitical position of the new Soviet Union, astride the Eurasian heartland, and thrusting toward both Western Europe and the mass-populated Asiatic coastlands, two basic strategic alternatives presented themselves.

One, which the communist leaders considered the superior, was the advance to the West. This meant the attempt to supplement Russian space, raw materials and manpower with Western machines and technology: in short, the communist conquest of Germany, and through Germany of Europe. This strategy was dominant in 1918, immediately following the Russian Revolution, and during the early 1920's. The defeat of the German revolutionary attempts in 1923 signified the temporary failure of this technological or Western strategy. It receded into the background until the favorable opportunity for its resumption in 1944.

From nearly the beginning, Lenin also reasoned that "the road to Berlin may lie through Peking and Calcutta." The cities were named in that revealing order. The World Revolution could triumph by conquering the huge territories, resources, and mass populations of Asia, and then taking the advanced nations from the rear as it were, after having cut off their bases of supply, reinforcement and renewal. "In the last analysis," Lenin wrote in 1923, "the outcome of the struggle will be determined by the fact that Russia, India, and China, etc., constitute the overwhelming majority of the population of the globe." This second (quantitative or Eastern) strategy was expressed by Lenin in his "Theses on the National and Colonial Questions," which were adopted by the Second Congress of the Communist International in 1920. From that time on, the program derived from the Eastern strategy went continuously forward, through defeat and victory, to the great triumph in China, and the present moves toward the neutralization of Japan and the conquest of Southeast Asia and India.

Lenin spoke of the mass populations of Russia, China and India as decisive only "in the last analysis." Similarly, Peking and Calcutta are referred to as stations on "the road to Berlin." The controlling event for the present period is the union of the Eurasian heartland, conquered by the 1917 Revolution, with technologically advanced Western Europe.

When reversed, the communist perspective reveals how the Asian-American strategy, carried to an extreme that meant the abandonment of Europe, could bring geopolitical disaster. Much short of the extreme it has a tendency to suck American power indiscriminately into the Far East. If this should lead to mass American land armies fighting in China, Southeast Asia and India, American power might be swamped and swallowed by Asia. The relatively minor war in Korea shows how easily and almost inadvertently this can happen.

Though a greater emphasis on the Far East than containment permits is desirable, this does not demand the commitment of mass American land armies to that region. In the Far East there exist nations which are anti-Soviet and which can become more so. Inside the communist controlled Far Eastern nations, or among exiles from these, there are many millions of individuals who are anti-Soviet. A correct American strategy will try to strengthen, aid and guide both such nations and such individuals. They could produce formidable land armies, both conventional and guerilla, with which American planes, ships and specialist units could collaborate when the occasions require.

The immediate Asian objective can hardly be the freeing of all East Asia from communist control or menace. After all, Soviet power is intrenched in Eastern Siberia and Manchuria, and has just conquered all China and Tibet. A defeat so vast as that in China is not upset in a moment. Along with strengthening Japan, the needed minimum is to prevent the consolidation of Soviet control in China, Southeast Asia and India, so that those areas, even if under conquering communist governments, will be not assets but rather liabilities in the total Soviet power system. This minimum is not beyond American capability. More is desirable, and more is not impossible.

4

To be convinced of the inadequacy of the Asian-American strategy, we need only imagine the state of affairs that would exist if it were carried out successfully. That would mean: a Japan rearmed and holding to a firm anti-Soviet policy; the suppression of communist partisans in Indochina, Burma, Malaya, the Philippines; Indonesia and India strengthened economically and free of major communist influence; anti-communist Chinese effectively opposing the Chinese communist government. Though such a situation in the Far East would certainly be better than the conditions of the present, it would be not nearly good enough. No fundamental problem would have been solved. The threat of the Soviet Empire, secure behind its ramparts, overhanging or even already possessed of Western Europe, and still pressing against the Asiatic Coastlands, would continue to be intolerable.

No American actions in the Far East—economic, political or military—hit the enemy where he can be really hurt. Whatever the United States does in that region, even with enormous expense and effort, affects only his periphery, pinches his fingers perhaps but does not get near a vital organ. The enemy himself knows this, as his handling of the Korean war has shown. By the Korean action, the enemy has bled American resources, pinned down a sizeable American force in a strategically pointless location, and diverted his opponent from the targets that count.

An Asian emphasis in American strategy leaves the enemy free to go about his principal and decisive business: the consolidation of the Heartland and of the surrounding Empire that has already been brought under his political jurisdiction. If a heavy Asian emphasis replaces the West European, then the enemy, hampered to his East, will be able to push out West or South.

In stressing the Far East, Senator Taft says that he is only insisting "that we apply to Asia the same basic policy which we apply to Europe. As I have said, that policy is to check communism at every possible point where it is within our capacity to do so." * If this is a correct statement, then he is only advocating the policy of containment magnified. In that case the criticisms of containment are doubly applicable, and the addition of the Asian-

* *Op. cit.,* pp. 111-2.

American strategy results merely in a more expensive way of being wrong.

5

We can interpret a combined program of the West European and Asian-American strategies in terms of traditional balance of power conceptions.

Up until this century, the preponderant weight of world power has for several hundred years been located on the continent of Europe. The idea of a "balance of power" has referred to a European political arrangement in which no single nation dominated the rest. Such an arrangement, consistently furthered by British foreign policy, was also of advantage to the United States. A balanced (disunited) Europe meant that there could be no effective European interference with the expansion of the United States first West and Southwest, and then to the Caribbean and out over the Pacific.

The result of the second World War, foreshadowed in the first, was to make the question of a purely European balance of power secondary. World politics no longer depend on the European balance, because the major part of world power is now outside of Europe. At the same time, Europe itself has been cut in half.

If we try to interpret the new situation in terms of the balance of power approach, we see that all Eurasia instead of merely its European peninsula is now at issue. Geographically, America, as an off-shore island, has much the same relation to Eurasia as Britain to Europe.

A balance of power does not now exist on the Eurasian continent. On the contrary, there is domination or potential domination by the single Soviet system. That this is true becomes obvious if we assume the power influence of the United States to be withdrawn from Eurasia. At once, probably without fighting, all of the Eurasian nations still outside of the Soviet Empire would have to submit to Soviet control.

Western Europe cannot balance the rest of Eurasia. A combined (Asia-Europe) program of containment would have the implicit objective of a power balance on Eurasia —in other words, the building of a counterweight to the existing Soviet power. If equilibrium could be reached in Eurasia, then America could control at will the inclination of the over-all world balance.

Geographically the Eurasian balance would take the form of an encirclement of the Soviet Empire: Western Europe on the West; Canada to the North (across the Pole); Japan, Formosa, the Philippines on the East; Southeast Asia and Indonesia at least held; India, Turkey and the various Arab nations on the South. The American island base would lie strategically poised to throw its weight toward either the Asian or the European shore.

The idea of such a Eurasian balance of power, amenable to American control, is attractive from an American geopolitical point of view. In fact, it would seem to be the almost inevitable long-run American strategic aim. Unfortunately, it is not a practicable goal in the present phase, nor in any event could it be achieved through a policy of containment. The immediately threatened encirclement is not by but of America.

The Soviet Empire is already so big that it can continue its internal development, encircled or not. Its present resources, population and strategic position are enough to over-balance not only Western Europe but all the rest of uncommunized Eurasia, even if the rest were strong economically and politically, and united in a firm policy of resistance to Soviet encroachment. Non-Soviet Eurasia is not at all, however, strong or firm. The Southeast (Indochina, Burma, Malaya) is under internal armed assault; the southern flank (India, the Arab nations) is very soft and probably a handicap; Japan begins remilitarization after the smashing of her military force and her armament industry; and the weakness of Europe we have already surveyed.

In general, the non-Soviet Eurasian nations are not going to make a great anti-Soviet effort merely for the strategic convenience of the United States. Yet the policy of containment offers them no positive goal to work toward.

From the idea of a Eurasian balance of power achieved through the encirclement of the Soviet Empire there is nevertheless a residue that is worth salvage. Though a

Eurasian balance cannot be achieved by the encirclement of the present Soviet Empire, it will become possible if the present Empire breaks up. Meanwhile, the immediate attempt at encirclement can be thought of more modestly as the search for favorably located military bases. In this sense the attempt has not been vain, and has already produced some excellent results. It is quite possible to establish valuable military bases in regions that count for little in terms of social power. The United States might get still better results if it thought about the encircling bases more consistently and coldly in military terms, with less ideological and sentimental admixture. For certain crises of the coming decade, airfields in Pakistan might prove more useful than a condescending pat from Nehru, and Spanish ports worth more than charming social relations with Third Force French politicians.

CHAPTER SIX

The East European Strategy

WE HAVE ALREADY OBSERVED * that the Soviet Union is
unlike any other political entity. It is a nation or rather
empire which issued from the Russian nation and empire, and it is at the same time the principal base of the
communist world revolutionary enterprise. This duality is
one key to the understanding of Soviet strategy.

The world revolutionary enterprise is conducted by an
"apparatus," an élite composed of "professional revolu-
tionaries" and "party activists." This élite is dominated by
its Soviet section which also functions as the governing
class of the Soviet Union. The leadership of the revolution and of the Soviet state are thus identical in fact
(though distinguishable in theory), with the consequence
that communist world revolutionary policy is ordinarily
equivalent in practice to Soviet imperial policy.**

* In Chapter III.
** If the first successful communist revolution had been in Germany or
Britain instead of Russia, then presumably the German or British section
would dominate the élite, the world revolution would have a Teutonic or

According to the Leninist-Stalinist conception, the success of the entire world enterprise depends upon the élite. The élite is the essential and deciding instrument of the revolution, and has priority over everything else: arms, territory, money, mass organizations, the forms of official power. In the strategy of the supreme leadership, the first task is *the preservation and strengthening of the élite.*

Preserving and strengthening the élite is a many-sided problem. During the war, its ranks were organizationally disrupted, and ideologically contaminated by too close contact with non-communist ideas and individuals. These weaknesses were energetically taken in hand by the supreme leadership. The frayed organizational threads were retwisted. Young recruits were carefully selected. Renewed emphasis on theoretical training went along with a series of purges in the arts and sciences. Political orthodoxy was narrowly defined and stringently enforced.

The principal territorial base of the élite is of course the Soviet Union itself, in particular Russia. The task of preserving and strengthening the élite means geographically, therefore, the defense and strengthening of the Soviet Union. The East European and Asian conquests, provided that these can be fully consolidated, offer the chance for the territorial extension of the primary base along with the incorporation of fresh strata in the élite.

English instead of a Russian flavor, and official anti-communist theorists would explain that communism is only the latest form of age-old German (or British) imperialism.

The preservation and strengthening of the élite as the principal instrument of world conquest, and the corollary defense and strengthening of the Soviet Union, are together a fixed and continuous principle of the communist enterprise. The present strategic phase, which began in 1944, can be specifically defined as that of *the preparation for the open stage of the third World War*. The objectives of this phase, which has both defensive and offensive elements, may be summarized as follows:

(1) The political, economic and ideological consolidation and strengthening of the entire Eurasian base, in such a manner as to insure its invulnerability to attack (whether in military or political form) and to prepare it for the phase of unlimited war to come.

(2) The weakening and subversion of all territories, nations and institutions which the communists do not control. In the present phase this is done primarily by political means, but also by limited and auxiliary military means when these are appropriate. This second objective is both offensive and defensive. Where a sufficient weakness appears, the communist drive carries through to conquest, and can either add territory to the Soviet imperial domain (as in the case of China) or establish an outpost in the enemy's rear (as in Travancore or Guatemala). Where optimum conditions do not develop, the operations can block effective war preparations by the enemy, establish internal vantage points for intelligence and sabotage, drain his energies and resources, and divert him

from any initiative against the main communist base.*

Because it is often overlooked, the diversionary function of many of the communist operations should be stressed. At the end of the war, the enlarged Soviet domain and the Soviet Union itself were in shaky condition. A bold anti-Soviet initiative by the non-communist world, military or political, would probably have resulted in the breakup of the new Soviet Empire and quite possibly in the overthrow of the Soviet regime. Even a mild initiative could have prevented the internal strengthening of the Empire. Therefore the communist leadership has sought to keep the non-communist nations busy on affairs that do not have an appreciable effect inside the Soviet sphere. Though the communist actions in Greece, Iran, Korea, Indochina, Malaya, Burma, Indonesia, Egypt, the Philippines, Guatemala and Berlin are not solely diversionary in intention, they are partly so. Their diversionary purpose has the advantage of being almost certain of success, even if other and more ambitious purposes fail. It should not be forgotten that the money, energies, supplies, manpower and blood that are spent in Korea or Indochina or Greece can never be used for the direct weakening of the Soviet Empire.

It is not only by shooting that diversions are created. When the communists injure the economy of France,

* In *The Struggle for the World* (John Day Co., 1947) and *The Coming Defeat of Communism* (John Day Co., 1950), I have discussed in some detail the present phase of Soviet strategy.

Italy, Brazil or the United States, the costs of economic repair are shunted aside from potential employment against the Soviet sphere. In the ideological field also, the communist apparatus fosters what might be called diversionary theories that help keep the opponent's lines of action directed toward targets other than the Soviet base. The theory that communism is a product of bad economic conditions is a good example of such an ideological diversion.

Even this brief summary of the present phase of Soviet strategy is enough to show that the policy of containment, whether concentrated on Western Europe or enlarged to cover Asia, is no great bother to the Kremlin. Indeed, the policy of containment is virtually a permanent offer to be diverted at the will of the opponent. All that the communist apparatus has to do is to stir up a little trouble anywhere in the non-Soviet world, or fan trouble already there, and it is assured in advance that non-communist resources will be channeled to that spot. Meanwhile, the communists are guaranteed immunity within their own base. What strategic prospect could be more comfortable?

2

Let us now approach the strategic problem by raising the question: why has the Soviet Union failed to move on

Western Europe during these years since the end of the war?

We know that the Soviet objective is world conquest. The Soviet leaders, believing that the absorption of Western Europe would ease their immediate difficulties and make their final victory inevitable, want to take over Western Europe, and intend to take it over. It therefore follows that they have not done so only because they have felt that they could not, that they lacked the capability.

It is certain that the Soviet leaders have not been (and are not) restrained by the military power available in Western Europe, because this has not been sufficient for them to take seriously. It is equally certain that no action or threat in the Far East has indirectly inhibited a Soviet move into Western Europe. The Kremlin has no reason to be alarmed at Far Eastern developments since 1945.

Three primary factors seem to have led to the Kremlin's negative decision:

First, the superiority of United States production and technology, and thus of the American armament potential.

Second, American superiority in atomic armament and in the ability to deliver atomic and other weapons of mass destruction.

Third, internal Soviet difficulties which arise from individual, class and national tensions. The Kremlin has feared and continues to fear that under the strain of general war these tensions might become so acute as to lead not only to military defeat but to the end of the Soviet system. That is why the Soviet leaders have felt it essential, before risking general war, to consolidate the internal regime of their Empire by a campaign of terror, indoctrination, and genocide.

The difficulties which arise out of national tensions have a special and direct strategic significance. Neither the present Soviet Empire nor the pre-1939 Soviet Union is a unified, cohesive national entity. They are aggregates of many separate nations each of which preserves its own individual national character. Within the Soviet Union proper the Russian nation comprises only a half or less of the approximately 200 million population. The other half is made up of Ukrainians (with approximately 35 million —of the same numerical order, that is to say, as France or Italy), Byelorussians ("White Russians"), Georgians, Tatars, Uzbeks, Azerbaijainians, and so on. These nations were originally brought under Moscow's rule by the Russian Czars. To them the communists have added China, Esthonia, Lithuania, Latvia, Poland, East Germany, Czechoslovakia, Hungary, Rumania, Bulgaria, Albania, East Austria, Tibet and North Korea.

All of these nations—those subjugated in the past by the Czars as well as those seized by Stalin—have their own languages, cultures, traditions, religions and histories. As nations, they all hate communism, which is counter to their religions and cultures. All or most of them also hate the rule of imperial Russian Moscow, whether or not communist. These nations are therefore more than a merely potential opposition to the present Soviet government. They exist now, as living historical realities. The Kremlin must, and does, recognize their existence, and takes account of them in day by day policy. The Kremlin realizes further that so long as these nations continue to exist they will aspire to political self-determination. They wish to be free from domination by an alien nation and culture, and they will act to achieve freedom if circumstances seem to offer them a chance.

General war would probably present such a chance. The first World War did so. At its tempestuous conclusion, all of the nations of Eastern Europe, including Ukraine, Byelorussia and Georgia, declared their independence and fought to break away from the respective empires—German, Austro-Hungarian and Russian—to which they had belonged. The same centrifugal tendencies were evident in the second World War, but were smothered by the combined policies of Stalin, Hitler and the Western powers. Even without general war, Yugoslavia broke away from Moscow's domination. The Kremlin feared, and fears, that in the event of renewed general war she will face a whole series of national revolts.

I have mentioned the fact that the West European (NATO) strategy applies without fundamental modification the experiences of the first two World Wars.

This archaism proves the old rule that a general staff always plans for the last war. But why should we not permit ourselves to be guided at least in some measure by what has happened *since* 1945? The events of these recent years bear much more directly on the problems of the future than does the record of wars fought under quite different world conditions.

Inasmuch as the Soviet Union would have conquered Western Europe if it could have done so, Western Europe can be considered to have been under attack since 1945, and to have been successfully defended. The defense has been accomplished by the existence of the American productive plant, the American nuclear and strategic air capability, and the internal tensions within the Soviet Empire. These three factors have thus proved their effectiveness in action, proved it by results. In spite of the absence of a powerful army on the Continent, they have blocked the Soviet advance westward.

All three of these factors are largely under the control of the United States, if the United States chooses to control them—much more directly under United States control than, at any rate, such matters as the state of mind of India or the military revitalization of Western Europe. The United States is able to maintain, develop and strengthen still further the world's greatest industrial plant. It can maintain and even increase its superiority in the application of scientific technology to weapons and to the means of delivering them to the enemy's base. If it resolves to do so, the United States can also nourish, enlarge, and bring to fruition the Soviet internal tensions.

Because these factors are subject to voluntary control, they can be made to wither as well as to grow. A given domestic policy, for example, can lead to the weakening instead of the development of the American productive plant. The proper application of scientific technology to armament requires more sacrifice of money and talent, and a more flexible and intelligent direction, than may be found or allotted. The exploitation of the internal Soviet tensions is impossible while the policy of containment endures.

Whatever the difficulties, it seems reasonable to seek guidance from the relevant past rather than from the possible future. To the extent that American strategy incorporates the three factors that have been noticed in this section, it is building on the rock of fact rather than on the sand of wishes. In themselves, these factors are not a policy, but they are materials from which the foundation of a policy can be laid.

3

In Chapters IV and V we reached the conclusion that both the West European and the Asian-American strategies, separate or combined, are inadequate. The critical analyses were not without certain positive results. In the course of argument there emerges the following list of tasks which the United States should seek to carry out:

(1) To prevent the absorption of Western Europe within the Soviet sphere;

(2) To continue the close links with Great Britain and the British Dominions, and the intimate cooperation with British sea and air power;

(3) To prevent the consolidation of Soviet rule in the Far East, notably in China;

(4) To block or at least hold up the communist drive into Southeast Asia and India;

(5) To strengthen the anti-communist nations of the Far East, especially the major nation, Japan;

(6) To guard and strengthen the home front;

(7) To strengthen and complete the military encirclement of the Soviet Empire by properly located air and sea bases.

Unfortunately, an amalgam of all desirable or indispensable objectives does not compose a grand strategy. If so, it would not prove very difficult to get agreement. There is not much dispute over what it is desirable for the United States to accomplish by its foreign policy. One faction does not propose something which the other rejects as totally wrong and counter to the national interest. Those who favor a greater Asian emphasis do not want the communists to take over Western Europe, nor would the champions of all-out for NATO rejoice at Soviet rule in India or Japan. The trouble is that no nation's resources are sufficient for it to be capable of doing all that it would be desirable for it to do. The strategic issue therefore always concerns priority, stress, timing, concentration. It is not so much what things must be done, as what order to put them in, what relative allocation of forces to make, what is to be rated dominant and what secondary.

Negatively, the United States seeks to remove the threat of Soviet world domination. Positively, the United States favors a world political order within which there would be a reasonable chance for its own citizens and all the peoples of the world to advance socially and economically without the continuous prospect of total war. Neither the West European nor the Asian-American strategy is able to achieve or even appreciably to further this general double objective.

Let us accept as a strategic axiom that first priority will be permanently assigned to the home front. Upon the home front's strength and well-being all else necessarily depends. Granted this axiom, it would seem to be indisputable that a strategy which had Eastern Europe as its geopolitical focus—Europe from the Iron Curtain to the Urals—would best serve the American objective. It will be argued that such a focus is impossible. Eastern Europe is controlled by the opponent, so how could there be an East European concentration? If a plan is impossible, what difference does it make whether it is correct? The objection is natural enough. For the moment, let us merely assume that an East European strategy is possible. If possible, its superiority is evident.

To carry out an East European strategy (if it can be carried out) would mean to bring anti-Soviet power to bear within the opponent's base, inside his lines, behind his front if it comes to a definite front, and across his communications. There can be no doubt that such action, or even the serious threat of such action, would have a much greater effect on the opponent than an act on his periphery or altogether out of his orbit.

So far as offensive action is concerned, action designed to weaken and defeat the opponent, an East European concentration is the only strategy that can accomplish anything at all. No matter what happens in the rest of the world, if the opponent remains untouched within Eastern Europe he will be able not merely to maintain himself but to develop his strength. Solidly planted within the Heartland, he can afford ups and downs elsewhere. Even major setbacks in the Far East would not be decisive for him. As both Lenin and Stalin have counseled, he can retreat today the better to advance tomorrow.

Untouched in Eastern Europe, he preserves intact the main body of his élite, upon which everything depends. He can employ secondary forces for action outside of East Europe. He commits little and therefore even if unsuccessful has little to lose. Through his world apparatus, the political nerve center of which is located within Eastern Europe, he constantly operates within the camp of his enemy, and exploits the rifts, troubles and disturbances that there arise. Separate counteractions to deal with each incident individually, as any anti-Soviet strategy other than the East European requires, are endless and hopeless, because the source of them all is left immune.

Power brought to bear within the main communist base, even within its outlying sectors, has necessarily the maximum effect. The closer to the brain, the greater the consequence of a given level of force. Even a small event inside the base can lead the opponent to withdraw from a major exterior campaign, as a minute electric current applied to a frog's brain compels the massive leg to jerk back. A large-scale interior action can achieve the opponent's overthrow—the liquidation of the Soviet regime—in a manner that is most efficient, least wasteful of life and of physical resources, and most promising for a civilized future.

Let it once more be repeated: it is impossible to defeat Soviet communism by either the West European or the Asian-American strategy, or any variant of them. I believe that these strategies cannot even defend Western Europe or non-communist Asia, nor in the long run the United States itself. Even if their defensive ability is granted, it is certain that you cannot defeat Moscow in London, Paris, New Delhi, and Chicago. It is suggested by the spokesmen of containment that we do not desire to defeat Soviet communism. Very well. But it is at least conceivable—even to containers—that the occasion may arise when general shooting will compel us to try to defeat Soviet communism. If so, where will the policy of containment be then? And where will be its attendant West European strategy, with or without its Asian supplement? The outbreak of general war would necessitate an immediate and complete policy revision. It does not seem much of a recommendation for a policy and strategy that they will have to be discarded as soon as the chips are down.

Even if we restrict our outlook to a defensive perspective, the East European strategy is plainly best—if it is possible. In order to defend Western Europe, NATO tries to build up a large land army within that area. There is continuous debate over what the NATO force shall do if the Soviet and satellite armies march West. Can the enemy be held at the Iron Curtain? at the Rhine? at the Channel and the Pyrenees? in Europe at all? Could a flanking redoubt be established in Denmark and Schleswig-Holstein? in south Germany and Austria? No solution looks too promising.

What if anti-Soviet force is developed within Eastern Europe? This would surely be the maximum deterrent to a Soviet move Westward: that is to say, it would be the best possible defense for Western Europe. If an attack were nevertheless made, such anti-Soviet force, so located, would be strategically the most effective possible weapon against the enemy. It would lie across the enemy's lines of communication, and extend even into the interior of his arsenals and headquarters. The mere threat of such a force would make the lines insecure, and would demand elaborate counter-measures. Ten men behind would be worth a hundred in front. The ten would indeed be worth several thousand, because if the fight has the appearance of a head-on clash between a united "East" (Soviet plus satellite armies) and a united West (inclusive of West Germany), then the battle will itself serve Soviet interests by tightening the links between Moscow and the Soviet imperial provinces. On the other hand, if from the start there are Balts, Poles, Czechs, Ukrainians—and Russians too—fighting *against* the Soviet command, then the effect of the battle will be to loosen the cement of the Soviet system.

I have been referring chiefly to the problem of Western Europe. The offensive and defensive superiority of an East European strategy is also evident in relation to the Middle or Far East and to the Americas. On the one hand, such a strategy alone can defeat or seriously weaken the Soviet state, because only such a strategy is directed against vulnerable points. On the other, an East European strategy, successfully carried out, would compel the Soviet energies to shift from external mischief to the defense of endangered positions at home.

4

If an East European strategy is desirable, is it also possible? Eastern Europe is Soviet-held. How can anti-Soviet force be brought to bear inside the enemy domain? In order to fight the Soviet power there must be armies. Where in Eastern Europe are anti-Soviet armies to be found?

Experience has already given a partial answer to these questions. During the past several years, United States and allied action has been effective against Soviet pressure to the extent that it has incorporated elements of an East European strategy. The strategic air force, able to atom bomb Soviet territory, has been a conscious "East European" element. Though it is not a unit that actually exists within Soviet imperial territory, the lines of force of the strategic air arm do reach inside. This has nearly the same strategic meaning as an actual Soviet location. There is no fundamental difference between an air squadron able to bomb Baku from a base in Britain, Africa or Maine and an artillery battery twenty miles away.

Though it has not yet been organized and guided, the latent force arising from the internal Soviet tensions is a second anti-Soviet element which operates directly from an East European location.

As for armies, there are organized armies in Eastern Europe—many of them. There is, for example, a Polish army that is larger than the army of any West European nation; and there are sizable Czechoslovak, Hungarian, Rumanian and Bulgarian armies. Who has decreed that the Polish army now commanded by Marshal Rokossovski must inevitably fight for the Kremlin? It will, if American policy forces it to. But there is not the slightest doubt that the great majority of Poles, including the Poles in Rokossovski's divisions, are still Poles and want to fight not for an imperial tyrant—foreign in nationality, alien in culture and religion—but for a free Poland. This is what they will do, if they are given any sort of chance. The same rule holds for the majority of Czechs, Hungarians, Slovaks, Rumanians and the others.

What if even a tenth of the money and energy that have been flung into the Marshall Plan and NATO had been spent on a campaign to win the allegiance of the captive armies of Eastern Europe? I find no reason to suppose that the anti-Soviet profits from that tenth would have been below the net gain from all the containment billions.

Nor is there any need to restrict our aim to the armies of the nations which have been subjugated since 1945. Within the Soviet armies proper, it is estimated that approximately 40% of the troops are non-Russian in nationality. There are Ukrainian units as large as divisions or even army corps, and smaller units of Byelorussians, Caucasians, and so on. Why do we take for granted that Ukrainian soldiers will fight for Russian communist imperialist Moscow, if they are given a chance to fight for a free and self-determined Ukraine? Neither Czars nor Bolsheviks have ever been able to complete the subjugation of the Moslem peoples of the Caucasus and the southeast.

Even the Russian soldiers should not be written off. Many of them are at heart more Russian patriots and human beings than communist imperialist robots. As men and as Russians they have more to gain from a fight against than for the communist regime, which is in the first instance a tyranny over Russians and Russia.

I wish to give an illustration of how an East European strategy translates itself into specific planning, and how strikingly such planning differs from the application of a West European strategy. This will be an illustration merely, and I do not intend to argue its practical merits. These could be determined one way or the other only by careful study. Nevertheless, the illustration is not chosen at random. It was devised and proposed, through underground channels, by a military specialist who is at present a general officer of one of the satellite armies.

According to his conception, if unlimited war begins two major actions should be immediately launched by the United States and its associated powers. The first is the massive bombing of the key Soviet military and industrial concentrations. The second is a parachute drop of a special force into a selected locality of Poland. This force would be a combined military-political unit of fairly large size. It would be highly trained—an élite group—and would consist primarily of Poles, with a fair number of Balts, Czechs and Slovaks also, some but relatively few Americans and West Europeans, probably no Germans.

This force would at once proclaim itself a resistance and liberation center, and would call for recruits from the entire region. It would seek to rally whole units from the Polish army, and a little later the Czechoslovak army, as well as individuals from among the Balts serving in the various Red armies. More generally it would be prepared to accept anyone who was ready to sign up, from Mongols to Russians to Rumanians. It would at once initiate a continuous political and propaganda campaign. At the first plausible moment, it would establish a provisional free Polish government, with other provisional governments for the neighboring nations following as quickly as might make sense.

Analogous actions might also be carried out in Southeastern Europe and in the Far East.

Such a plan would require elaborate preparation on both its technical and its political side. After thorough examination it might be found incorrect or not feasible. But is it fantastic, simply not worth considering? From a point of view hobbled by containment it will undoubtedly seem so. How, one may wonder, would the Kremlin judge it? How would the Kremlin rate a unit of this sort, so situated, as against NATO divisions massed in front of the Red Army at the Elbe or the Rhine?

I do not stress in this context the "Resistance" groups and activities that might be developed in Eastern Europe. Such groups already exist on a restricted scale within at least several of the nations. The skeleton of the Ukrainian Insurgent Army, which became a formidable anti-Bolshevik as well as anti-Nazi force during the latter part of the war and for a year or two thereafter, still exists in the Ukraine and still carries on limited activities. Partisan groups are also operating in Czechoslovakia, Poland, Rumania, East Germany and perhaps elsewhere. Individual secret "resistants" are to be found throughout the Soviet Empire. The presence of this anti-Soviet Resistance is itself a further demonstration of the realism of an East European strategy.

A Resistance, however, is a special corps composed of a special type of human being. Except in times of major crisis and social turmoil, the active Resistance can never involve directly more than a small percentage of the population. At the same time the effectiveness of a Resistance depends upon its having behind and below it the sympathy, good will and political solidarity of the majority of the local population. Without that, the Resistance cannot solve even its technical problems of survival and combat. If it does not disappear altogether, it tends to degenerate into a handful of paid agents or a mere outlaw gang.

Though the development of a Resistance is certainly one of the measures by which an East European strategy would be carried out, I have wanted to fix attention on a broader problem. Beyond the relatively narrow Resistance framework, the strategy aims toward the great armies already organized in Eastern Europe, and toward the entire peoples and nations. I remember when one evening in Stockholm I asked an Esthonian exile leader whether any active Resistance groups were still operating in his homeland. He replied: "The Esthonian nation is the Resistance." He meant, of course, not that the people as a whole were busy at underground activities but that in its captivity the nation persists as a living reality, with a soul, a will to freedom, immune alike to the terror and the seduction of the Kremlin.

An East European strategy cannot be carried through in the military and semi-military spheres alone. Military strategy is dependent in the end on policy. An East European strategy presupposes a general policy which would in decisive respects break with the policy of containment that has prevailed since 1947. This I call *the policy of liberation*.

A policy of liberation would apply in all major spheres: military, economic, psychological, diplomatic, political. It would not be easy or cheap nor could it promise immediate and magical results. It would not require that Western Europe and the Far East should henceforth be left out of account, or even that the bulk of anti-Soviet effort, quantitatively considered, should be directly applied to actions affecting Eastern Europe.

What the policy of liberation first and essentially means is a particular focus or perspective. Granted always the axiomatic priority of the home front, it means the view

138

that *the key to the situation* is what happens and what can be made to happen in Eastern Europe, Europe from the Iron Curtain to the Urals. So far as possible, therefore, actions in every sphere (military, psychological, diplomatic, economic) and every geographical area will be selected and judged in terms of their direct or indirect effect on Eastern Europe. A free Rumanian regiment training and marching under the Rumanian flag, with the immense moral effect which this would have on the captive Rumanian army and nation, will be thought to outbalance an unfavorable editorial in *The New Statesman and Nation* or *Le Monde*. A high staff position for General Wladislaw Anders, which while utilizing his talents and his combat experience of Soviet armies would do him and his nation appropriate honor, will be recognized as worth a Soviet denunciation in the United Nations. Diplomats will be more anxious to attend the celebration of a Lithuanian national holiday than the Soviet Embassy receptions in honor of the Bolshevik Revolution against democracy.

In the remaining chapters of this book I shall examine some of the consequences of the adoption of the policy of liberation with its corollary East European strategy. This examination will be neither complete nor dogmatic. If liberation is to become the policy of the United States and ultimately of the entire free world—and it is not impossible that it will—much labor will be needed to translate it from general idea into detailed reality. Within its fundamental perspective, there is room for differences of opinion, even wide differences, about how it should be carried out. My own answers to many concrete questions may be quite wrong, even if I am right about the problem of general policy. I want only to show how one thinks under the guidance of the policy of liberation, what sort of problems arise, and how some of these may perhaps be solved.

CHAPTER SEVEN

Land, Sea, Air

ACCORDING TO PREVAILING DOCTRINE, the United States should try to maintain a "balanced" military establishment. As a formal principle, this can hardly be challenged. The trouble lies in the interpretation of "balance."

The United States military establishment is administratively organized along the lines of medieval chemistry. Three of the four medieval "elements"—land, sea, and air (with fire omitted)—are represented in the three services: army, navy, and air force. With this structure, the complete military force is believed to correspond to the "three dimensional" character of modern warfare.

Accepting the tripartite division, the easiest interpretation which can be given to "balance" is approximate equality among army, navy and air force. Even this interpretation is not quite clear. You cannot equate ships numerically with planes, or either with tanks. Nor does it seem to make sense to equate the number of men in each service. The equation is therefore understood in financial terms: equality means that army, navy and air force will be allocated approximately the same amounts of money in the annual budget.

To justify this impartial financial equality, a long string of arguments has been trotted out. We can't risk putting all our security eggs in one military basket, says one school of prudent counsel. Contemporary war is fought and won in all three dimensions, so we must have superiority in all three arms, say the advanced thinkers. We can't rely on sea power because ships near shore are at the mercy of land-based air power, and besides ships can't reach into the Heartland. Air power may be indispensable, but it can't hold territory. Korea proves again that air power can't win final victory. The Luftwaffe couldn't take Britain. Each arm has its appropriate function, and to neglect any one of the three for the sake of the others is to upset the security equilibrium and court disaster. And so on.

Although these arguments have been ingeniously made, and annotated with learned accounts of the wars of this century, I suspect that they have not been the deciding factor in favor of the "balanced force" theory. There is a different kind of consideration that inclines Washington toward "balance."

In the first place, the equality solution accords with the liberal and bureaucratic cast of mind. The liberal always insists that "there is some truth on both—or all—sides." As seen by the liberal, advocates of the unilateral primacy of land, sea or air power are dogmatists and probably fanatics. Each puts forward a strong case. The liberal makes an "objective" compromise by combining all three "truths" in the concept of "the balanced force." This suits the bureaucrat (who is often the same person), because what the bureaucrat wants above all is to avoid having to take responsibility for a clearcut decision. Taking his seat on the balance theory, the bureaucrat figures that he can't go wrong.

The balance theory is also the least troublesome from the standpoint of practical politics. Each of the three services aims to get for itself the maximum cut from the military budget pie. The Joint Chiefs of Staff have a natural tendency to quiet the squabbling by recommending equal thirds. This is a still more plausible solution for the average member of Congress, who has not studied military history or theory, and who feels conflicting pressures not only from the services but from constituents and lobbies as well.

Since the first World War, the principal debate has been over the function of air power. There are no longer many open spokesmen for the traditional theories of land or sea supremacy. Those who adhere to such views in their hearts find it expedient to use the balance concept as a diplomatic cover.

At the same time it may be remarked that when things get tight the balance is usually upset in favor of the army. For several years after the second World War, the financial treatment of the three services was kept roughly equal. With the Korean war and the NATO rearmament of Europe, the air force began to be favored in budget allocations for a frequently postponed future, but at the same time the share of the army in current expenditures began to rise. A feeling of security springs most readily from a big mass of "soldiers," men organized to fight on Mother Earth.

2

A correct decision about the structure of a nation's military establishment will presumably rest upon certain objective facts. Most relevant among these would seem to be: the facts of geography—location, size, resources, population; the level of technology and the nature of the economy; the position, capabilities and weaknesses of the enemy; and the relative efficacy of different weapons.

Even without an extended analysis based on such facts, I think that there is reason to doubt the equal balance theory. In any field, the mark of effective strategy is always concentration. In politics and business and sports as well as in war, the able strategist never spreads—that is, diffuses—his power all over the lot. He gathers his forces together, and brings them to bear on a particular point at a particular time. It is impossible to be equally strong everywhere at all times and in everything. Nor is it necessary. All that is needed is to be sufficiently strong in the relevant items at the critical moment and place. A baseball team doesn't space its heavy hitters evenly up and down the batting order. A football team doesn't try to open up the entire opposing line. A business firm requires not merely millions in the bank but alert executives who are ready to use the millions at just the moment when a big opportunity arises, or is made. A political candidate does not win a campaign by talking on every subject in the encyclopedia, but by hammering away at the few issues which really move the electorate and touch the soft spots of his opponent.

It is not different in military affairs. The great strategist is a dogmatist. He does not open his mind equally, in liberal fashion, to every opinion and every factor. He searches for *the key to the situation*. When he believes that he has found the key he concentrates every available force on the key, and lets subordinates or the enemy worry about the remainder.

The military history of peoples and nations yields little evidence for the equal balance theory. Sparta preserved her sturdy independence for more than five hundred years without altering her concentration on solidly trained foot soldiers. She finally lost out not from neglect of cavalry and the sea but because of archaic tactics that could not match the more flexible maneuvers of the infantry of Thebes and Macedon. Not until Athens put her entire reliance on the sea—so much so that on one occasion her people left the city empty and made the fleet their nation—did she become great. Attila did not worry about a navy or an infantry. For four hundred years, England did well when she stuck to the sea, and her first switch to the land—in the mass English armies of the first World War—was the beginning of her downfall. Napoleon or the Kaiser might have won domination of a unified Europe if they had been content with their natural element of the land and had renounced until due time their dreams of maritime glory.

The balance theory treats all three services alike. No favorite is played. In the eyes of the budget, the three are equal—equally important, equally decisive or rather equally undecisive. One consequence of this military egalitarianism is to make it almost impossible to have a unified national war plan. What happens in practice is that the army develops a plan based on the assumption that land warfare is decisive; the navy, on its premise of the supremacy of sea power; and the air force, in air terms. Victory through land power, victory through sea power, victory through air power. The Joint Chiefs of Staff—who are not a true General Staff because each of the Joint Chiefs continues to be a member of one of the separate services—then sew a patchwork from the three cloths.

It follows as a further corollary that the equal balance theory leads to waste and inefficiency even beyond the military normal. Each of the three services strives to be self-sufficient, and to be strong enough to win the war on its own, with only auxiliary help from the other two. Each separate service is trying to be stronger than any other military establishment in the world. This attempt is needless as well as impossible. The rational aim would

146

be to have a military force which in its integrated entirety would be stronger than any other in the world.

Let me add that I am criticizing the theory of a balanced military establishment only if "balance" is interpreted to mean "equality." There is another sense in which a "balanced" establishment is certainly desirable: where "balance" means a due and proper proportion, as established by geography, capabilities, and objectives, among the various elements that make up the total military force. Balance of this kind would not only permit but ordinarily require inequality rather than equality in the assignment of money, men and material to the different services.

3

From the point of view of world geography, North America is an island lying off the shores of the great Eurasian land mass. To be an "island" today has a dual meaning. As in the past, it means to be washed by the water, the sea; and it now means also to be washed by the limitless ocean of the air. More open even than the sea, the air ocean is a highway and a theater of combat, leading everywhere, in every direction.

The United States, together with its allies, has under control or can easily acquire a sufficiency of convenient sea and air bases. With the rapid advance in the operating radius of ocean (sea and air) craft, a multiplicity of distant bases becomes, moreover, a lessening requirement.

Though the United States is perhaps not the equal of several other nations in pure science, it stays in the front rank with the help of foreign-born scientists who become residents or citizens. It is far beyond any other nation or combination of nations in scientific technology, and in the mass industrial application of scientific technology. It has a population trained to work in an economy of highly developed mass industry, and accustomed from birth to a culture of machines and rapid motion.

The United States has a relatively small percentage of world manpower, and no historical tradition of permanent mass land armies.

The principal base of the enemy is inaccessible by sea. The direct approach to it by land is long, slow and costly. The enemy controls, directly or indirectly, relatively large numbers of men. His technology and industry, and the technological training of his population, are at a quantitative and qualitative level much below that of the United States.

The enemy is vulnerable within his base. He is vulnerable politically, as was discussed in the preceding chapter, and also militarily and economically.

There is a generally accepted belief that a "primitive" economy is less vulnerable to strategic bombing than an advanced economy. Understood with some qualifications, this is probably true. For example, a society based upon an agricultural village economy, like most of India or

148

China, will not be much affected by the destruction of this or that village, whereas all Britain would be hurt by the successful bombing of Sheffield or Newcastle. When this belief is extended to the comparative form—the more advanced an economy, the more vulnerable—and when it is concluded therefrom that the American economy is more vulnerable than the Soviet, it seems to me mistaken.

The Soviet economy is no longer, of course, "primitive." At the same time, it is not, taken as a whole, advanced in the rounded sense that applies to the United States or several of the West European nations. Soviet economy is uneven and distorted, highly advanced along some lines, in others still backward and primitive. It has lost the local self-sufficiency of a primitive economy without having gained the adaptive flexibility of an economy which has reached a balanced stage of advanced development.

The Soviet Union, for example, has made its agriculture dependent on tractors, but at the same time has only a relatively small number of factories able to turn out farm machinery, few developed sources of petroleum, and badly organized facilities for manufacturing and distributing spare parts. The Soviet railways are perennially overloaded, and there is no cushion in the form of a great automotive industry with an attendant road system. Scattered thickly over half of the territory of the United States there are tens of thousands of large and small factories, almost all with first class tools and machines, and a trained labor force to draw from. It would be very difficult to destroy the ability of the United States to make any given war implement, because in an emergency, if one set of plants doing a particular job were eliminated, it would always be possible to adapt and convert other plants elsewhere. The Soviet Union has no such industrial reserve to fall back on.

It would seem probable that the carefully planned destruction of a small percentage of the Soviet industrial establishment, while it might not lead to capitulation, would remove the Soviet potential for aggression.*

Even so summary a review seems to lead unavoidably to the following conclusion: the United States, in the light of its own position and resources as well as the nature and position of its opponent, should put its primary military reliance on air power plus scientific technology. (I include within "air power" guided missiles, rockets, and similar devices.) A military plan so oriented means that the United States thereby chooses its own ground, leads from strength, and has a chance to make the most of the opponent's weaknesses. Sea power, in the narrow sense, cannot reach the opponent, and therefore cannot be made the primary concentration. To try to match him

---

* In connection with the last war, it should be recalled that: (a) Hitler did not carry out a systematic plan of strategic destruction; (b) the Soviet Union was supplied by the United States and Britain with immense quantities of the products of advanced industry; (c) the Nazis could have defeated the Soviet Union if they had not been politically insane.

150

with land power would be to play his game on his terms.

A military program oriented primarily on air power (plus scientific technology) does not mean that sea power and land power are to be eliminated. It means that sea power and land power are not permitted to develop "their own" independent plans. Both are brought under a single integrated conception, the first and essential aim of which is domination of the air ocean and its use as a route for the transport and delivery of power at will. Sea power continues to have traditional tasks in connection with the control of sea lanes, but its supreme task becomes that of helping in the conquest and use of the air ocean— by support of air bases, and by providing platforms from which air devices can be launched. Whether aircraft carriers still make military sense, and if so what size and kind, is a technical question which I am not equipped to answer. Without technical knowledge, one may conclude that if carriers do make sense, then they should exist for the sake of the planes and rockets which they can launch, not the planes and rockets for the sake of the carriers.

Under a doctrine of air power concentration, land armies would continue to have many functions. There will always be fighting on land. As in the case of sea power, however, the most important job of the land forces would come to be understood as the support and furtherance of air control and air utilization. Particular attention would turn toward troops who by training and mission would be closely related to air power: defensively as guards (in the widest sense) of air installations; offensively as specialized air-borne and parachute units—winged soldiers, air cavalry, able to raid two thousand miles behind the lines tonight and be gone before the defense arrives tomorrow, ready to liberate a Siberian slave labor district this week, spearhead a revolt in the Caucasus the next, and blow up an enemy powerhouse over the weekend.

Against the doctrine of air power concentration, it is argued by the defenders of the equal balance theory that recent experience has proved air power to be incapable of winning a definitive victory, of reaching a *decision*. This is shown, it is said, both by the second World War and by Korea. Planes can't "hold territory." Whatever bombing may succeed in accomplishing, the job has to be finished up on the land. Air power may be necessary to victory but it is not sufficient. In the Korean war, the United States has had air supremacy and has not won.

Although these arguments are not without substance, I do not believe that they justify abandonment of the air power doctrine for the equal balance theory. The anti-air power arguments always fail to make reference to the most important factor of all: the capabilities and geopolitical position of the United States itself. The United States does have, qualitatively and quantitatively, the capability for air domination. It is not capable of matching the Soviet Empire on land. Conceivably the United States will be defeated by the Soviet Union no matter what kind of military plan the United States adopts. But defeat is absolutely certain if the result depends on the size of the two land armies. Inasmuch as Washington cannot possibly have as large an army as Moscow, it would do better to quit trying, and to spend its money and energy on something that it can have: namely, air and technological superiority. The United States has to take a chance on these even if they aren't much good. In fact, however, they are quite good enough.

In estimating what air power can do, we should remember that no nation has yet made a real air power concentration, nor has air power been allowed to operate with the advanced weapons and equipment that are already available. Suppose that before 1939 Germany had actually concentrated on an autonomous and supreme air arm, instead of making the Luftwaffe an adjunct of the land army. Is it so clear that Germany would in that case have lost the Battle of Britain? Korea tests nothing fundamental, not only because the air power assigned there is limited in number, quality and armament, but because victory has not been an objective in Korea and thus could hardly be achieved no matter what air power did.

But let us assume that air power cannot of itself bring final victory. It remains true that victory is impossible *without* air power, and that a concentration on air power is therefore still justified from an offensive standpoint as well as the best insurance for defense. If air power has not brought victory in Korea (or not been allowed to), it is also true that *unless* air power had intervened, the communist forces would have conquered the entire peninsula within the first two weeks. No one will claim that the few troops who arrived in the early days could have stopped the communists without help from the air. In general, if the United States has air superiority, it is not going to be defeated even if it cannot completely win. This is not such a trivial assurance.

Those who are skeptical about air power should reflect on the meaning of the absence of air power. What would an overwhelming army be worth today if it were tied to the ground, deprived of accompanying air power? What would the world's largest navy amount to if it couldn't get above the surface of the sea? There doubtless remain some odd places and special terrains where air power doesn't count for much. These are strategically unimportant in the world power struggle. No major conflict is thinkable any longer without air power. If air power cannot by itself seize and hold territory, it can make territory useless for anyone else to hold, and it can open the road for its seizure by troops that from a purely land criterion are of modest number and weight.

Let us make a further assumption counter to the extreme form of the air power doctrine. Let us assume that the total anti-Soviet military establishment must be "balanced" in the equality sense, with a land army on a quantitative par with the air force. In the long run, and for the complete task, this may be true, or approximately so. It still does not follow that the United States must supply

the bulk of these land troops, or that the United States'
own military establishment must itself be equally balanced.

The correct way by which to assemble the mass land
armies of the anti-Soviet coalition is through the pursuit
of an adequate and dynamic policy. The manpower for
these armies exists—much of it at least partly trained and
ready to come together at the proper summons—in Western Europe, Asia, and also in Eastern Europe. If American policy cannot gather allied mass armies from these
sources, then it is probable that the Soviet Union can
never be defeated, or the world preserved in the end from
total Soviet conquest. Surely there can never be enough
American soldiers to overrun and police Eurasia.

There is no reason to pay the smallest attention to
blackmail talk about "using the masses of Europe and
Asia as cannon fodder." The cannon fodder in Korea has
come for the most part from Texas, Illinois and New
York rather than from Europe or India. Everywhere today Americans occupy or share the posts of greatest present and potential danger. The percentage of casualties in
the planes that may bomb Baku or Magnetogorsk or Moscow would much exceed those of any land army in any
land battle. If Europeans and Asians are not willing to
sacrifice and if necessary fight for their own liberties, then
they will lose them.

The policy of containment leads to military plans
which place their primary emphasis on land armies. Dur-

ing the past few years this has been proved by experience. For the NATO coalition in Europe, for the semi-United Nations coalition in the Far East, and also for the United States itself, the land armies and their relative weight within the military force have been increasing. This shift toward the land is indicated by a revealing verbal symptom. A few years ago, popular discussions of military strength centered almost exclusively on "squadrons," "wings," and nuclear weapons designed to be carried by planes or guided missiles. In the containment-NATO atmosphere, talk has come to revolve around "divisions," "army corps," and "tactical" nuclear weapons suited for employment by land artillery.* Meanwhile, the air procurement program is "stretched out" indefinitely into the future.

In general, the concentration and reliance on land armies seems to be the solution most favorable to the enemy. If it is possible to justify it with respect to the total force of the anti-Soviet coalition, it is surely the most wasteful and least effective answer to the narrower problem of the American military establishment. It disregards the geography, resources, economy and relative population of the United States, the present stage in the development of military science, and the strengths and vulnerabilities of the enemy.

---

* To an amateur, the United States Army's new 80 ton atomic land gun sounds rather silly. It is so awkward to transport and to set up that the enemy must be expected to take the initiative in massing his troops obligingly within the very limited range of its expensive muzzle.

156

The fact that a military concentration on land armies follows from the policy of containment is an additional heavy count against that policy. The fact that a policy of liberation, with its strategic focus in Eastern Europe, leads naturally to a concentration on air power is a strong argument in its favor.

CHAPTER EIGHT

The Primacy of Politics

Two UNDERLYING THEORIES have greatly affected United States policy toward communism and the Soviet Union. On first thought, the two seem inconsistent with each other. In practice they go readily together. Both are widely believed and daily acted on by government officials. So deeply are they imbedded within the public as well as the official mind that unless they are torn out they may be expected to continue their baneful influence even when the policy changes. No matter how plausible these theories may seem, no matter how authoritatively pronounced or popularly accepted, both are demonstrably false and demonstrably injurious. They are not merely "doubtful," "only partly true," or "open to question." They are flatly false, and have been proved false by historical experience.

The first is the theory that "communism is the product of adverse economic conditions." The second is the theory that "in the last analysis, fire power decides." I shall discuss, and refute, them in that order.

Logically, the theory that communism is a product of adverse economic conditions is a derivative of the more general theory of economic determinism: the doctrine that economic conditions are the fundamental cause and explanation of all that happens in history. Economic determinism was a belief held irregularly by Marx and more constantly by his colleague, Friedrich Engels. It has characterized the tradition of "orthodox" Marxian thought. By a curious irony, this belief, abandoned long ago by the communists, has found a lodging in the main fortress of the anti-communist world, in the United States.

The American form of economic determinism affirms two basic propositions which though psychologically related are logically independent of each other. One is that bad economic conditions cause the growth and victory of communism. The other is that an improvement in economic conditions will stop communism. This double belief constitutes the avowed motivation for the Marshall Plan, the economic parts of the Mutual Security program, the economic aid to Asia and South American nations, the Point Four ("technical cooperation") program, the famine relief programs, and so on. American officialdom has backed up its doctrine to the tune of tens of billions of American dollars.

Mr. William C. Foster was expressing the official doctrine plainly when as Deputy Director of the Economic Cooperation Agency (Marshall Plan) he said: "Europeans do not yet have a real good living standard, a standard which insulates them from communist subversion from within." Harry Truman used to sum it up in the phrase "stomach communism."

It is not difficult to see why this doctrine is attractive to a rich and lazy nation. What it really suggests is that we can buy our way out of the present international crisis. If we spend enough money—which is after all the least of human sacrifices, especially when one has so much—then we can dispense with brains and will, courage and endurance and blood.

Lenin, on his side of the revolutionary fence, confronted early in his career a similar belief, which he called "the theory of spontaniety." An opposing faction within the radical movement argued that revolutionary ideas and organization would arise "spontaneously" out of the daily grievances and struggles of the workers. Lenin insisted, in contrast, that the revolutionary theory and program had to be brought to the workers from "the outside," that workers would never spontaneously advance beyond "trade union consciousness"—that is, the effort to improve their wages and working conditions. As for revolutionary organization, that also could not develop spontaneously among workers and peasants, but only as a result of the deliberate action of professional revolutionists.

Lenin, the leading expert on the matter, was unquestionably correct. Communism is at one and the same time a set of beliefs and an organized apparatus. The beliefs are intricately elaborated, difficult and sophisticated. The disciplined organization combines the complexities of an army and a conspiracy. How could such an organization, holding such beliefs, arise "naturally" out of adverse economic conditions? Bad economic conditions can stimulate certain vague mass moods—desire for better things, apathy, frustrated resentment—and under some circumstances can lead to sporadic waves of unrest and objectless revolt. But how could "conditions" give birth to the subtleties of Dialectical Materialism and the delicate maneuvers of the United Front?

The contemporary facts are well enough known, and should not be ambiguous. Communism comes to a nation not spontaneously but through the activities of a trained, centralized international enterprise with headquarters located in the Soviet Union and agents operating everywhere on earth, in the best and worst economic conditions, among the poorest and the most wealthy. The only element of the economic determinist view which need even be considered seriously is the modest suspicion that the communist enterprise finds bad economic conditions a favorable soil for its crop, and that conversely communism cannot produce a harvest from good economic conditions. Many find this restricted doctrine so persuasive that they think it almost self-evident, but it too is false.

To say that communism flourishes under bad economic conditions and is stopped by good economic conditions means to assert a positive correlation between communism and bad conditions. If this correlation holds, it would follow that the strength of communism within nations, classes and individuals would be roughly proportional to the badness of the economic situation—that is, to poverty. The richer a nation, class or individual, the higher its standard of living, the less communism; and vice versa.

The fact of the matter is that we do not find any correlation whatever, positive or negative, between the strength of communism on the one side and economic conditions on the other. Communism has grown strong in both rich nations and poor, among more and less favored classes. Communism has failed to grow strong in other nations and classes both rich and poor.

Czechoslovakia was the richest nation of Eastern Europe. From shortly after the first World War the Czechoslovak Communist Party has been, both absolutely and relatively, the largest of Eastern Europe. Czechoslovakia, moreover, succumbed to communist rule without direct armed intervention from the outside. If it is argued that she was under heavy Soviet pressure, which is true, it should be recalled that the pressure was considerably less than was put on Finland—a much poorer country which has not succumbed to communism.

Turkey is a poor country, incomparably poorer than, say, France or Italy. After its defeat in the first World War, and the consequent loss of its battered empire, Turkey was in particularly bad economic straits. From early in the 1920's, Turkey has had no communists at all, other than a few Soviet agents and spies. France and Italy have had and continue to have mass communist movements.

The communist movement in Brazil has been relatively one of the two or three strongest in Latin America. Brazil is relatively one of the two or three richest Latin American nations. Though India and China are both incredibly poor, India is the poorer. It is China that the communists have conquered. Spain is one of the two poorest countries of Western Europe, but for fifteen years Spain has not had a major internal communist problem. Spain's partner in poverty is Ireland, whose perpetually "adverse economic conditions" have not bred a hundredth the number of communists that has sprung from the vastly richer economic soil of France. Portugal, richer than Ireland but much poorer than France or Germany, has never had a genuine communist party.

In all of the Arab nations the mass of the population is abysmally impoverished. The communist development differs in them all. In Saudi Arabia and Jordan there seems to be little communist strength; in Egypt and Iran there is much. There is more communism in Israel than in Saudi Arabia, Iraq or Jordan, though Israel's economic level is far higher. Insofar as they differ economically, India's level is above Pakistan's. Communist strength is conspicuously less in Pakistan than in India.

If we state the problem in terms of "advanced" (industrial) vs. "primitive" (agricultural) economies, we find the same lack of correlation between communist development

163

and economic conditions. Communism has conquered or grown strong in advanced economies (Germany, Czechoslovakia, France), in primitive economies (China, Bulgaria, Indochina) and in the intermediary economy of the Russian Empire. Communism has been relatively weak in other advanced economies (England, the Netherlands, the United States) and in other primitive economies (Saudi Arabia, Turkey, Thailand).

If we use classes and individuals rather than nations as our point of reference, it can once more be shown that communism is not a function of poverty. No matter how it may seem "logically," it is just not true that communism makes its primary appeal to the poorest classes or the poorest individuals. Though the communist enterprise is often able to manipulate the poorest classes, its recruits and close sympathizers usually come from social strata substantially above the bottom.

For many years in the United States, polls with the response divided according to income level have been taken on attitudes toward communism and specific communist-connected issues. They have shown a correlation which is the reverse of what our official economic determinists believe to be the case. The higher the group income level, the more favorable the attitude toward the Soviet Union and communism.

The poorest third of the population has always been overwhelmingly anti-Soviet and anti-communist. Millionaires and the children of millionaires, like Frederick Vanderbilt Field and Corliss Lamont and George Marshall, have gone along with the communists. The percentage of communist college professors is higher than the percentage of communist railroad laborers, small farmers, or ditch diggers. Hollywood and Broadway actors, producers, writers and directors, drawing thousands of dollars a week, have flocked into the communist movement, but not steel workers or coal miners. There are relatively more lawyers and dentists than truck drivers within the U.S. communist orbit. Alger Hiss was not one of the grossly underprivileged.

There are variations from country to country. Within some nations the communists have gained control of the major trade union organizations. This does not mean, however, that the majority of the workers within those organizations are procommunist. Besides, the trade unions never include the poorest strata of the community. Nowhere, East or West—certainly not in Russia itself—do we find that the strength of communism is in any sort of direct ratio to economic level.

Asia is not different in this respect from Europe or the Americas. The lowest classes of the Asian countries do not become communist. It is almost physiologically impossible for them to do so. To be a communist involves a kind of surplus activity, mental and physical, over the bare business of living. The masses of India, China, Pakistan and the Arab nations live a desperate, diseased, perpetually famished existence. They have neither time nor energy nor thought for the luxury of communism.

Although communism within these countries has won some exceptional individuals from among the peasants and soldiers, it has made its greatest headway with the younger generation of the native upper and middle classes, with professionals (lawyers, journalists, doctors, teachers, etc.), and with bureaucrats. Amusingly enough, the Asian universities, schools and hospitals supported by the money of the great American foundations, from Beirut to Lahore to Peking, proved easy recruiting grounds for communism.

The French physicist, Fréderic Joliot-Curie, the Anglican Dean of Canterbury Cathedral, the Italian physicist Bruno Pontecorvo, the famous German playwright, Berthold Brecht, the fabulously successful painter, Pablo Picasso, the prosperous British attorney, D. N. Pritt, all these and tens of thousands of communists and fellow-travelers like them, have a good deal more to lose than their chains.

2

So much, then, for the theory that communism is the product of adverse economic conditions and that it fades away under good economic conditions.

I repeat: communism is a disciplined, centralized world enterprise, geographically based on the Soviet Union but operating everywhere. It is a power, that is, a *political,* apparatus. Communism does not mysteriously "arise" in this or that nation, class or individual. It *is brought* by the agents and influence of this dynamic enterprise.

When working on a nation, the communist enterprise finds it advantageous to exploit whatever rifts, conflicts and tensions may exist there, or which it can stimulate. These rifts may be of any sort—ideological, racial, religious, linguistic, cultural, and also, of course, economic. The rifts and tensions do not in themselves specifically favor communism. They constitute a weakness in the social fabric. Any other conscious, disciplined organization could also exploit them. In Germany between the two world wars the Nazi organization proved more successful than the communist at doing so, as Perón was in Argentina—or, though this analogy is not complete, Roosevelt-Truman in the United States.

With respect to the non-communist world, the communist enterprise is nihilist. That is to say, its aim is to destroy the structure of that world. Within every nation there is always a variety of rifts, tensions and conflicts. Therefore a shrewd nihilist organization will always find a lever to pull. What determines whether communism (or any comparable enterprise) will become strong and eventually conquer is not the presence of the rifts, but the character of the leadership that opposes the attempted subversion.

The historical evidence shows that the major condition for communist success is a wishy-washy government, a government (or governing class) that cannot make up its mind with respect to the political issues, that cannot *choose*. This major condition is *political*—not economic, material, cultural or ideological. It does not even seem to make much difference what choice is made ("reactionary" or "progressive," Right or Left, war or peace) so long as there *is* a choice. Men must feel that they are going somewhere, that they are moving in some definite direction. If their existing leadership can't give them that feeling then they will turn to one that will.

In Russia in 1917, the crucial issues were the war, food, and land distribution. The Kerensky government couldn't make up its mind to fight or not to fight, to distribute or preserve the large estates. The government was full of high-minded sentiment, and had the allegiance of many intelligent, able individuals. But it fell to the drive of the Bolsheviks with not much more than a whimper. If not the Bolsheviks, it would have been Kornilov.

For Czechoslovakia from 1945 on there was just one crucial issue: to line up with Moscow or with the West. The Beneš-Masaryk government did not answer the problem one way or the other. It did not declare unequivocally either for or against Moscow; it was going to be a "bridge" between East and West that would prove the two to be reconcilable. The end came with the communists in power and Masaryk jumping out of a window. It may be argued that Czechoslovakia is so small compared with the colossus to its East that the outcome was inevitable no matter what the government did. Possibly so. Yet Finland, which is weaker than Czechoslovakia in population, industry and resources, was confronted with a much harsher choice. Finland answered firmly not only in words but with guns. Finland, though harassed and circumscribed, is still free. Greece also gave a flat answer; and Greece also is free.

In China the problems were many and immense. For the period following the war, probably two were crucial: the land and the communists. The peasantry, the great majority of the population, could be held only by a dynamic land program. To the threatened advance of the communists a Yes or No answer had to be given: to crush the communists or submit to them.

No answer was given to either problem. In spite of all the talk and small scale action here and there, the government of Chiang Kai-shek never did initiate a dynamic land program on a broad national scale. So far as the communists went, the answer changed from month to month: bottle them up, resist them, capitulate, form coalition goverments, "democratize". . . . The decisive period, which coincided more or less with the presence of General Marshall in 1946-47, was squandered in the Kerensky-like plan for a coalition government—a pseudo-policy which was in reality the abandonment of all policy.

In the case of China, the political failure which was the condition of communist success cannot be attributed solely, perhaps not even primarily, to the Chinese Nationalist government. After the long years of the Japanese

War and occupation, the attrition of open and disguised civil war, and the liabilities carried over from its more distant past, China could have met its two crucial issues only with the help and firm guidance of the United States. Neither help nor firm guidance was given. The influence of the United States was used not to promote but to prevent a firm policy. The specific objective of the Marshall mission was to block any program to crush the communists: to prevent Chiang, that is to say, from giving a clear answer, the only possible answer, to the communist problem. The United States cannot avoid a full share in the responsibility for the communist conquest of China.

This kind of paralyzing intervention by the United States has not been confined to China. India today is analogous to China in 1946. The same two issues are crucial: the land, and the threat of Soviet-backed communism. For India, the problem of the land is both technological (new agricultural methods) and sociological (a new system of ownership). In both aspects what is required of the Indian government is a program able to arouse the enthusiasm of the active elements of the masses. The problem of communism is both internal and external. Its solution, as in the case of China, demands the crushing of the internal communists, and, internationally, an unequivocal stand on the anti-Soviet side of the world struggle.

Nehru's government answers neither one problem nor the other, or rather gives a dozen different partial answers

170

as mood and occasion shift. Nehru plays around with local land reform projects, technical or social, just enough to get headlines in the domestic and world press. Toward communism he shifts almost by the hour: a few local communists in jail here; there, a delegation singing the praises of Mao Tse-tung; a self righteous speech condemning both capitalism and communism, and an ambassador proclaiming the virtues of Stalin; slander about internal American conditions while eating American grain; sabotage of anti-communist operations in Korea while protesting India's serene non-partisanship; fulsome welcomes to Soviet "cultural" visitors and a parliamentary speech condemning communist "materialism."

Granted India's condition, the strength of India's communists and the weight of Soviet pressure, Nehru's present course indicates the communist conquest of India within the next decade. The United States, far from acting to shift the direction, works as if to confirm it. Proceeding on the economic determinist theory of "stomach Communism," some aid, principally food, medicine, and other immediate relief commodities, is shipped in. A few small technical projects along lines of agricultural improvement, river control and the like—all good enough in their limited terms but without political force—are started. Meanwhile, political relations have been put into the hands of people like Eleanor Roosevelt and Chester Bowles, persons with the same kind of wishy-washy, vague, indecisive temperament as Nehru's own. Instead

171

of clarifying the mind and stiffening the backbone of the Indian government, the representatives of the United States play up to its most confused and debilitating qualities, shamelessly flatter Nehru and his family, soften at Nehru's criticism the previous mild anti-communism of the U.S. propaganda services, and set out to conquer the heart of the East by sending diplomats' children to native schools, confessing American sins, and riding to the Embassy on bicycles.

The State Department's procedure in France has been basically the same. The communists are the most powerful French political movement. If they cannot today take over the government, or do not wish to, they are able to cripple any major French action that they sufficiently oppose. In particular, they can prevent France from functioning effectively within an anti-Soviet military coalition. The internal Soviet-directed communists are, then, one of the crucial issues now faced by France. There are two others: escape from production-stifling cartelized economic forms, and rapid advance toward European economic and political unification. Toward all three problems, the kaleidoscopic French governments since 1947 have shown the same indecisiveness and straddling, the same inability to answer and decide, that are the classic conditions for the success of communism.

The United States, in accordance with its economic determinist premise, has pumped huge quantities of material aid into France. After five years and at least five billion dollars, everything is just where it started from. This should not be surprising, because the essential condition has been left untouched. To throw the communists back takes more than money, bread, cotton, and textile machinery. It requires first and primarily a firm, clear policy, a decision, definite answers to the basic questions. This is the requirement that the wobbling Third Force, centrist French governments by their very nature cannot meet. These governments depend for their existence on balancing opposing forces, not on solving problems.

The State Department has encouraged the continuation of just this kind of weak, indecisive, temporizing French government, and has actively fought against the emergence of a government that might be able to be firm, to give answers to questions—which in France during this period could only have meant a government under General De Gaulle.

Just why the State Department has so often favored policies and governments which prevent a determined fight against communism is something of a mystery. I believe that it is partly because weak governments are easier to manipulate. The fact that they may not be worth manipulating is forgotten in the relief at being assured of a compliant answer in public, and a supporting vote at international meetings. The second reason for the preference is, I think, that the State Department has itself had the same political style as the governments which it has favored, and has been temperamentally inclined toward the same kind of straddling, no-decision policies.

My aim here has been to establish the following:

(1) Adverse economic conditions are not responsible for the origin, growth or victory of communism.

(2) The principal condition for the success of communism is political—indecisiveness on the part of government, the failure of a nation's leadership to make up its mind with respect to the crucial issues.*

The evident, practical conclusion that the primary method of meeting communism must be political, not economic, does not imply opposition to economic aid for the non-communist nations which need aid. We may choose to give aid out of purely humanitarian motives, or because we think it good business. Let us then give aid, but let us not suppose that by doing so we are going to stop communism.

In the struggle against communism economic measures are useful only to the extent that they promote anti-communist political or ideological results. This lesson we can learn from the communists, who inside or outside the Soviet Empire never take any economic action for its own sake, but always with an eye toward the political effect which the action can serve.

---

* Of course, a weak government is not in itself a *sufficient* condition of communism. Weak governments can last a long time if they are not strongly challenged. Other forces than communism can make the challenge.

The "agrarian program" has been the principal feature of communist propaganda and action in Asia. Many non-communists are deceived into thinking that the purpose of the agrarian program is to meet the problems of the agrarian economy. This is not at all the case, as a careful examination of the program will prove. Land distribution as advocated by the communists results in most countries in the breakup of farms into unworkably small holdings. The purpose of the communists, however, is not economic but political. They aim through their agrarian program to stir the peasants into action under their leadership, and to weaken the prestige and power of social classes that are opposed to communism. It does not trouble them that their program means a lower instead of increased pro-duction of food. They have in any case no intention of leaving the land under the individual proprietorship of the peasants. When a communist government is firmly installed, it begins the process of collectivization. This is once again an economic measure used for a political end—the *de facto* expropriation of the peasantry in order to destroy the socio-economic basis from which the peasants might function as an opposition social group.

If economic aid is to further an anti-communist pur-pose, the same rule must be followed in reverse. It can't be just a question of immediate relief or (as the Marshall Plan has seemed to the European masses) of patching up the old machine. Aid must be, or must seem to be, related to large programs and lofty goals, to a crusading spirit and exciting changes, and it must especially be presented in such a way as to appeal to the youth—to offer ambitious young people something to do now and the hope of still greater things that will become possible tomorrow.

A principal reason for the lethargy of such countries as France and Italy is the plain fact that able young men and women have nothing to do, and are given nothing to look forward to. The politico-economic situation offers them hardly any jobs with a chance for fame and fortune, and for the feeling of a significant task accomplished. Under the policy of containment—that is, a policy of indefinite stalemate—the billions of dollars of aid alter very little this dismal and negative prospect. For it to change appreciably, the youth must be able to see vast new possibilities ahead: the real development of Africa as a European frontier; an economic unification of Europe, with the economic structural revolution which this would bring; the lifting of the Iron Curtain (that is, the liberation of Eastern Europe), with the immense opportunities which would thereby arise for West European brains and industry; the reopening of the Far East to an era no longer of colonial exploitation but of cooperative economic advance.

3

A young friend of mine who spends his time trying to promote what he believes to be a major political warfare project managed early in 1952 to get an appointment with

General J. Lawton Collins, Chief of Staff of the Army. While my friend made his presentation, General Collins listened with what seemed to be attention, understanding and sympathy. After he had finished, General Collins leaned forward and said politely:

"Yes, young man, but in the end isn't it all a question of fire power?"

This question was not a personal foible of the Army's Chief of Staff. It is an expression of the second false theory that lies back of American thinking on problems of foreign policy. In the last analysis, in the showdown, fire power decides. Diplomacy, economic aid, propaganda, treaties and Leagues of Nations are all very well for shadow boxing. When it comes to the main bout: fire power, that's what counts.

The theory of the supremacy of fire power is, naturally enough, most widely held among the military. It is often found alongside the economic determinist theory. As applied to the struggle against communism, the two might seem to be incompatible: if communism is a product of bad conditions and is stopped by improving economic conditions, then it would seem that victory or defeat for communism is not going to be decided by fire power. Nevertheless, the two theories function in a single mind as a kind of first and second reserve. The economic determinist theory backs up the economic operations of peacetime. Officially speaking, all problems are going to be solved "without war." The fire power theory rests in deeper echelon, ready to be brought forward when the switch to shooting takes place.

The fire power theory seems to be very practical, realistic, down-to-earth. To many persons, it also seems to be substantiated historically by the history of the United States. United States diplomacy, policy and treaties during the past century have not been very wise or adroit. In all of the wars from the Mexican War on, the United States, either alone or with allies, has brought superior fire power to bear, has always won, and is still going strong.

No matter how realistic the fire power theory may seem, it also is demonstrably false. It is not false in quite the same way as the economic determinist theory. That is just false, mistaken, from beginning to end. The fire power theory is false when stated as a general historical hypothesis, but it is true or approximately true when formulated with suitable restrictions. It is true usually of an engagement; often true of a battle; sometimes true of a campaign. It is seldom true (without modification) of an ordinary war, and probably never true of a civil war or of a long drawn out contest, comprising several wars and many modes of struggle, between two great nations, peoples, religions or systems.

In a single engagement, the side that brings the greater fire power to bear on the contested spot usually wins. In a full scale battle, the situation is not quite so simple. It is still true that the side which brings the greater fire power to bear on the key point will probably win. That is not necessarily the same thing as to say that the side which *possesses* the greater fire power will win. Superior maneuvers, strategy or politics may mean more effective employment of quantitatively inferior fire power.

The case of a mutiny or civil war is much plainer. If the fire power theory were true, no revolt would ever have succeeded. The established authorities are always initially superior in fire power to the rebels. By political means, daring, and cleverness, the rebels seize or immobilize part of the fire power.

Even if it is true that a war in being is decided by fire power, that is still a conclusion of derivative importance. Which side will act in the way that will produce its own power potential? If the United States is physically and economically capable of having the largest quantity of fire power in the world, it does not follow that it will so act as actually to have it. The United States may prefer to make television sets rather than war planes.

What fire power did the Bolsheviks have prior to 1917? A few hundred revolvers, and a little home-made dynamite. If Lenin had shared General Collins' belief about fire power, he would have taken down his revolutionary shingle and gone fishing. Lenin believed in the supremacy not of fire power (or of economics) but of politics and political will. He knew that fire power was also important, but he aimed to appropriate his adversary's fire power and to use it for his own political purposes. This is what he did.

In 1944-45, the Allied armies under Eisenhower in Europe held the greatest quantity of fire power that had ever been assembled. Theoretically, that fire power could have been employed to prevent the Soviet conquest of Eastern Europe and the consequent strategic unbalancing of Eurasia. Stalin, though relatively much inferior in fire power, was superior in political knowledge and political resolution. Stalin and the communist generals were therefore able to immobilize and even thrust back Roosevelt and the allied generals.

Immediately following the war, the United States, by virtue of its monopoly of nuclear weapons, had an incomparable advantage in effective fire power. Stalin replied to the nuclear weapons not with counter-fire power but with politics. He seduced the nuclear scientists, and paralyzed the will of the opposing leadership. The atomic bomb became even more useless than the gold buried under Fort Knox—the gold at least serves a positive purpose so long as it is believed in. The bomb became a source of embarrassment and guilt-feeling instead of an asset. It was transformed from a symbol of material power into a proof of political impotence.

With respect to nuclear weapons, conditions have not greatly changed. Although the United States still has overwhelming superiority in nuclear armament,* it can-

---

* I am not convinced that the Soviet Union has any nuclear weapons effective for war-making purposes. Even if it does, it is so far behind the United States as to be altogether outclassed.

not make any use of this superiority—it cannot even threaten in a voice that will be taken seriously. Why should I worry about my opponent's bigger fist, if I can talk him out of punching? The bombs dropped with such a fanfare from public relations officers on the Nevada flats do not kill any communists, and do not even frighten them while they remain sure that the United States lacks the will to employ them in combat.

That this is the case is proved to them daily in Korea. It is mere pretense to declare that "military considerations" have dictated the failure to use nuclear weapons in Korea. The enemy knows, the allied governments know, and the American leadership knows that from a purely military point of view nuclear weapons would unquestionably have been used—at the very least for experimental and training purposes. The reason for not using them is political. The wiles of the opponent, bellowed from the Moscow and satellite radios, echoed from the communist and fellow traveling press, sugared over by the Partisans of Peace, shrewdly playing on the weaknesses and fears of our allies, reaching through the minds of agents or dupes directly into our own councils, have succeeded in neutralizing our superior fire power.

Perhaps the most spectacular of all recent demonstrations of the inadequacy of the fire power theory was the Koje Island affair in the spring of 1952. Tens of thousands of communist prisoners, totally disarmed, without a shred of fire power, had been brought to Koje Island and there placed behind barbed wire fences guarded by thousands of soldiers with almost limitless fire power at their disposal. Within a few months the prisoners were in virtual control of the island. They had set up their own courts, execution chambers, government, communications. For many weeks, they had sovereignty over the interior of the compounds. They seized and held hostage the enemy commanding officer. They negotiated as equals, and exacted humiliating terms and confessions from their fire powered but paralyzed captors.

The explanation for the Koje affair, one of the most disgraceful in American history, is purely political. It has obviously nothing to do with fire power. On the communist side, there was a superior policy carried out with knowledge, resolution and determined leadership. On the American side, there were only brave soldiers, uninformed of the nature of the enemy, and castrated by a disastrous policy and an irresolute political leadership.

An analysis of the theory of the supremacy of fire power leads to the same conclusions that we reach after analyzing the theory of the economic source and cure of communism. The theory is false, and most damaging in its practical consequences. Our age is the age of the primacy of politics. Without correct policy, money and arms are nothing. Equipped with an adequate policy, with a political goal and the political will to pursue it, men will find— or take—the money and arms.

CHAPTER NINE

Is Political Warfare Possible?

THREE FACTS are the only triangulation points by which a firm course of foreign policy can be charted in our time:

(1) The world political system is in the midst of a transformation which goes beneath and beyond the limits of the national and colonial order that prevailed during the past several centuries.

(2) For the period of this transformation there is no clear line between war and peace. There are only different forms and stages of the continuous struggle for survival or dominance in the developing world system of the future.

(3) The primary mode of the struggle is *political warfare*.

By "political warfare" I refer to methods of struggle other than those of formal military warfare, insofar as these methods are guided by a strategic objective.

Although they differ on its role, all military strategists agree that the advent of air power has added a "new dimension" to warfare's traditional land and sea. Outside of communist circles, few military strategists or governmental leaders yet comprehend that another, a fourth, dimension, more novel and decisive than the third, has simultaneously appeared. Air power alters the tactics and mechanics of war, but does not bring any qualitative change in the nature of war, nor reach into any new layers of the human mind and spirit. Political warfare demands a radical shift in both conception and practice.

In thirty years (1921-51) Soviet-based communism conquered China, the most heavily populated country on earth. This immense victory was won almost entirely with the weapons of political warfare. The amount and scale of formal fighting, the equipment used, and the casualties in the field were negligible in relation to such a goal. It is doubtful that the communist High Command spent as much as a half billion dollars on the whole thirty year campaign, certainly less than a billion. From 1946 to the end of 1952 it took more than seven billion for the French to maintain a shaky stalemate in Indochina. The United States has used much more than a billion merely to keep a thin line open to the single city of Berlin.

In achieving the conquest of China, Stalin's political warfare included the following measures:

(1) A clear policy, first laid down in theses adopted by the Second Congress of the Communist International (1920). This policy had the conquest of China as its unequivocal objective, in order both to add China's weight to the communist side of the world balance, and to de-

prive the Western powers of a major reserve of resources and manpower.

(2) The organization of a trained cadre, an *apparat,* which became the brain and backbone of the Chinese revolution. This was done by sending instructors and organizers from the Soviet Union into China, and by training tens of thousands of Chinese in special Soviet schools.

(3) Carefully regulated Soviet pressures and infiltration, open and disguised. The Soviet emissaries ranged from military advisers to saboteurs to economists to spies to engineers. The infiltration extended deep into Chinese society. The pressures gradually gained strategic domination of the land approaches to China: Outer Mongolia; then Sinkiang; and, in the next to last phase, Manchuria.

(4) Flexible Soviet diplomacy, which demanded here and yielded there, made or broke a treaty as opportunity suggested.

(5) Skillful political handling of the Japanese war against China. The Japanese invasion of the mainland (Manchuria, then China proper) was parried in such a way that the threat to Soviet territory was minimized, the Chinese Nationalists undermined, and the Chinese communists strengthened both materially and morally.

(6) Shrewd exploitation of internal Chinese tensions. Agrarian (peasant) discontent was mobilized under communist leadership. Wide strata of the intellectuals, professionals and bureaucrats were penetrated ideologically.

185

Many of the merchants and businessmen were neutralized by fear, indirect bribery or Pan-Asiatic and anti-foreign slogans.

(7) Paramilitary and military operations, tailored to Chinese geographic, economic and social conditions.

(8) Soviet manipulation of the Western powers, first by entangling them in a Soviet-sparked "anti-Japanese front" and then by snatching key concessions from the conference tables at Teheran and Yalta.

(9) Immobilization of Western public opinion by psychological means. In order to conquer China, the communists had to prevent effective interference by the Western powers, in particular by the United States. This was accomplished by a psychological operation which exercised a controlling influence on Western, especially American, opinion concerning China, and by the actual penetration of relevant Western institutions, both governmental and private.*

2

During the past few years the term "psychological warfare" has become familiar in the United States. Many popular articles have been written about it. Everyone seems to be "for it," and to agree that we ought to carry

* The *Hearings* on the Institute of Pacific Relations, conducted by the Internal Security Subcommittee of the Senate Judiciary Committee, and the Report of the Committee on those *Hearings* are an incomparable source of detailed information on this psychological operation, as well as a remarkable study of communist procedures in general.

on vigorous psychological warfare against communism and the Soviet Union.

As a matter of fact, what professes to be psychological warfare is being conducted on a rather large scale. Probably more than half of the budget of the Department of State goes to "PW," as psychological warfare is known to its familiars. It is the chief business of the Department's Division of Public Affairs, and occupies much of the time of its intelligence section, the Office of Intelligence and Research. The other divisions of the State Department frequently try their hand. In 1950 the Army set up a new psychological warfare branch. The Army's special research organization, the Operations Research Office, spends many of its millions on psychological warfare, as does the Air Force's special organization, the Rand Corporation. The Air Force also works in the field through its Human Resources Research Institute. Other Departments of the government are often drawn in. The Central Intelligence Agency has many psychological warfare tasks which are not publicly defined. In connection with the Marshall Plan and the Mutual Security Agency, huge and expensive psychological projects have been attempted abroad. All of the government's psychological warfare operations are supposed to be "coordinated" by the Psychological Strategy Board, which works under the direction of the National Security Council.

Outside of the government proper, the field of psychological warfare has been yielding a heavy crop of varied organizations, some semi-official, some altogether private, which function both at home and internationally. Prominent among these has been the complex which includes the National Committee for a Free Europe, the American Committee for the Liberation of the Peoples of Russia, the Committee for a Free Asia, and various auxiliaries such as Radio Free Europe, the Crusade for Freedom and the Free Europe University in Exile. American help has been given to such groups in Europe as the "Peace and Freedom" movement which now functions in seven nations (the French *Paix et Liberté* has been the most widely publicized), the German League for Struggle against Inhumanity and the Free Jurists Association, the European federalist groups, and so on. American trade unions, especially the American Federation of Labor, have promoted the development of the non-communist International Confederation of Free Trade Unions. Private American corporations, foundations and individuals have been trying to conduct psychological warfare in their own way and on their own account.

The United States is now spending what must total well over a billion dollars yearly on these products that are sold as "psychological warfare," and advertised, by those who are paid to turn them out, as high grade anti-communist medicine. Let us take a look at the contents as well as the label. Is this American brand of "psychological warfare" the genuine article? Does it actually function within the great new dimension of contemporary international struggle?—in other words, is it an authentic form of *political warfare?* Or is it, perhaps, a substitute for political warfare?

Soviet political warfare is an expression of *the will to defeat an enemy*. American "psychological warfare" is for the most part an expression of the wish to be loved. In that contrast is summed up the fact that American psychological warfare is in reality not political warfare or, indeed, warfare in any sense. The object and purpose of war, whatever its form, is the defeat, partial or total, of an opponent. If an activity does not have that purpose, then it is not warfare, no matter what it is called. Some of the things done under the American program have the aim of weakening or checking (though hardly defeating) the Soviet Union. Most have a mixture of motives, among which the wish to be loved—so profound a characteristic of American culture—is the most prominent.

A large part of American psychological warfare consists of an "information and education" program, carried out through radio, lectures, movies, books, libraries, student and teacher exchanges, reciprocal traveling, and so on. Its avowed purpose is to clear up "misunderstandings" and to correct "misinformation" concerning the United States. Its message (the Campaign of Truth vs. the Big Lie) is roughly the following:

> The communists say that we are imperialists, reactionaries, warmongers and racialists. They tell you

that we exploit workers and farmers, lynch Negroes, drop germs on peaceful peasants, and plan to make an American colony out of all the world that we leave unatomized. It is not fair for them to say such things, and they are just not so. We Americans want peace and prosperity for all, and it is slander to suggest that we would ever start a war under any circumstances. We hardly ever lynch Negroes any more, and they can now even eat in restaurants and railroad dining cars—at least in some parts of the North. With the way progress is going, they will soon be able to register at hotels. We have never sought territorial gain, except where it is a question of defense or helping a young nation to grow up. We are ready to pay out billions of dollars to bring the benefits of our prosperity and way of life to everywhere in the world. At home, our workers are the richest and happiest anywhere, with cars and bathrooms and vacuum cleaners and television, and it is not true that they are exploited, and they want to be friends with everybody. As for our farmers, why should they want war when they have such big barns and fat cattle and broad fields? Our University graduates are not barbarians, like the communists say, but they really like art and culture, and we are going to prove it to you by sending over *Oklahoma* and John Gunther and *Porgy and Bess* and *Captain from Castile* and *Quo Vadis* and *Life's* reproductions of paintings. And our leaders are so friendly that they are ready to call you by your first name ten minutes after meeting you.

The curious assumption seems to be that others will love us if they see us as we really are. And why? The only evident reason is that they won't be able to help loving us because we so want to be loved. In their ardent youth, Americans have not yet learned the tragic lesson that the most powerful cannot be loved—hated, envied, feared, obeyed, respected, even honored perhaps, but not loved. Was not the Renunciation of Love the first step in the search for the Treasure of the Nibelungs?

Displayed on the high and opaque fence that surrounds the United States Consulate at Basra in Iraq I saw big photographs of mid-Western farms bursting with new buildings, machinery and prize cattle. Are the starving and diseased Iraqi peasants and laborers who shuffle past that fence going to love us because they see that our farmers are so rich and well fed? The Marshall Plan propaganda has told the workers of France and Italy that the American standard of living is four times higher than the Soviet. Will those French and Italian workers, in their unrepaired, cold and grimy homes, love us because our workers ride to work in big cars and have steak three times a week? Will the prospect-less European student love us because our writers can get $2,000 an article from the *Saturday Evening Post*? Will ordinary Rumanians and Balts and Russians love us because we endlessly repeat that we will never take the offensive against the regime that crushes them?

How preposterous to suppose that political attacks based

on "the Negro question" can be quieted by quoting statistics on lynching and subsidized housing. The fact is (if
it were relevant) that American racial tolerance is well
above the world average. Not only is the United States far
more tolerant and assimilative than countries like South
Africa and Australia, with their special problems, but it
is more so than many non-White nations such as Japan,
China and India.* The Japanese speak contemptuously of
the United States as a "mongrel nation." A Chinese family
regards a child of mixed Chinese and White parentage as
an outcast. Indians are so obsessed by the color question
that young bachelors advertising for brides specify light
color as a prime requirement. This is the fact, but facts
have little to do with the political passions that are merely
using the Negro and similar issues as adventitious
symbols.

It is not only the information and education part of the
American program that expresses the passionate wish to
be loved. "Friendly acts" are constantly being performed
with the apparent expectation that these will lead to feelings in the recipients if not of love at least of gratitude. It
is evidently forgotten how much more bitter it is to
receive than to give.

In the late summer of 1952, Moslem pilgrims piled up
in Beirut on the way to Mecca. The United States ran a

* Most inhabitants of India are of course themselves to be classified scien-
tifically as Whites. Subjectively, however, Indians usually identify themselves,
though ambivalently, with non-Whites.

"Magic Carpet" of airplanes to transport thousands of them free and comfortably. Undoubtedly this was done on the inspiration of one of the psychological warriors. Operation Magic Carpet was presumably part of the campaign to "win the Moslem world to our side."

It would be churlish to object to this performance. Humanly speaking it was a pleasant thing to do. It probably gave the pilots useful training. And I imagine that it made the Beirut authorities happy by getting the penniless pilgrims off their doorstep. At the same time it was almost certainly useless as a psychological warfare action. In the Moslem religion and culture, the feeling which Christians designate as "gratitude" does not exist. Islam teaches that all things, good and bad, come from Allah. The planes that took the pilgrims to Mecca appeared and functioned by and solely by the will of Allah. For that, the pilgrims no doubt gave due praise to Allah. It would have been sacrilegious and indeed unthinkable for them to feel thanks, gratitude or obligation toward the American pilots, generals or diplomats. These were the instrument that Allah happened to choose—in this case, *despised infidels*. If they felt anything toward the Americans, it was probably distaste and ironic contempt.

So far as psychological warfare goes, the Arabs have been impressed lately not with the sporadic friendly acts but with the increasing signs that the infidels have grown weak and cowardly. The Christian dogs slink away from

193

their possessions without a fight, and cringingly wait on a Persian fanatic in his bedchamber . . . .

3

"Psychological warfare" is a more imposing name for what used to be called "propaganda." Propaganda means the use of the media of communication for the purpose of influencing groups of people in accordance with pre-determined political goals. The field of propaganda, though wide, is only a part or subdivision of political warfare. The outline given above of the methods used by the communists in the conquest of China shows that many of the forms of political warfare are outside of what would usually be classified as propaganda.

It follows as a practical conclusion that the objectives of propaganda cannot be successfully set beyond the range of general political warfare. The limits of political warfare are in turn fixed by a nation's over-all foreign policy. Since 1947 the United States has pursued the policy of containment. American political warfare and American propaganda have therefore necessarily been confined within the perspectives of containment.

This relationship between part and whole is by no means self-evident. It seems to many persons that there is no reason why propaganda cannot perfectly well follow one policy while ordinary diplomacy, commerce or military preparation follows quite another. It just does not work out that way. If the propaganda is completely out of line with actions taken in other fields, then no one believes the propaganda, and it has no effect. When Hitler went into Byelorussia and the Ukraine in 1941-2, his propaganda said that he arrived to free the peoples from Russian Bolshevism. Byelorussians and Ukrainians were ready to welcome him as liberator. But when his Nazis treated the Byelorussians and Ukrainians as subhumans, the propaganda was disregarded. It serves no purpose for the Voice of America or Radio Free Europe to tell the Czechs and Poles that America stands for their freedom if at the same time the State Department keeps officially implying that it is always ready to negotiate with a "sincere" Moscow or Peiping on the basis of the present boundaries of the Iron Curtain. Because containment offers no solution for the chief problems of Europe and Asia, and only the prospect of eternal enslavement to the peoples of the Soviet Empire itself, there can be no effective American propaganda before the policy of containment has been abandoned, in action as well as in words.

The United States has made a certain effort to get around the dilemma thus indicated by what amounts to a trick. It has been thought possible for the nation to have two policies: a publicly avowed "overt" policy—the policy of containment, negotiations and faith in the United Nations; and a secret or "covert" policy which would be much more strongly anti-Soviet, and would in some respects approximate a policy of liberation. The overt policy would govern diplomacy, official propaganda, and behavior at conferences. The covert policy would be carried out by special unacknowledged agencies, secret agents, and private organizations.

In the modern world it is of course normal that some operations should be "covert." This is necessarily the case with many intelligence activities. There is a recognized covert type of propaganda, known technically as "black," where the true source is hidden. From the outset, many of the communist operations have been covert. In the attempted American trick, however, there is something quite different from these other instances.

In standard practice, the overt and covert operations are designed to serve the same strategic and policy objectives. This may not always be obvious, inasmuch as one set may be acting as a deception maneuver to conceal the other. Basically, they nevertheless push toward the same goal, and thus supplement each other.

What one section of the American government has tried to set into motion is a program of covert operations organized in terms of a different policy from that which guides the government's overt actions. Analysis and experience prove this double deal to be impossible. One of two results follows: either the desired effect of the covert operations is canceled out by the counter-influence of the overt actions; or the covert operations degenerate into irresponsibility and adventurism.

Many private or semi-official activities among exile

groups have been caught on one of these horns. The Free Europe University in Exile, for example, was established through American support in 1951, with its resident center at Robertsau, near Strasbourg. The student body is drawn from the exile youth of the East European captive nations. Implicit in the idea of this University is the perspective of liberation. In fact, the only motive for founding it would seem to be that of preparing selected young persons for the time when their countries will again be free. In practice, the general influence of the policy of containment has smothered the potential dynamism of the University in Exile beneath attitudes of timidity and negativism. In the appointment of staff and tutors, the relations with the neutralist French authorities, the selection of visiting lecturers and the guidance of special studies, the political content is diluted with the sterile waters of containment. The institution tends to develop as a charity school instead of a fighting instrument of political warfare.*

The so-called Kersten Amendment to the Mutual Security Act of 1951 authorized the expenditure of up to $100 million "for any selected persons who are residing in or escapees from the Soviet Union, Poland, Czechoslovakia, Hungary, Rumania, Bulgaria, Albania, Lithuania, Latvia, and Estonia, or the communist dominated or communist occupied areas of Germany and Austria,

---

* I am a founding Trustee of the Free Europe University in Exile, and make these comments from direct acquaintance.

and any other countries absorbed by the Soviet Union either to form such persons into elements of the military forces supporting the North Atlantic Treaty Organization or for other purposes. . . ." The debate over this provision showed that Congress' intent in passing it was to initiate the formation of exile military units. This purpose, like the University in Exile, presupposes the perspective of liberation, and goes counter to the policy of containment. Therefore the containment-committed Administration denied the plain meaning of the Amendment (when the Soviet spokesmen attacked it in the United Nations) and sabotaged it in action. The whole business was surrounded by super-secrecy, in order to hide the fact that nothing positive was done except to give a little financial aid to refugees.

The Committee for Free Asia, to cite a third example, was organized in 1950 with large funds at its disposal. Presumably it also is supposed to be working unofficially toward the goal of liberation. In two years all that it accomplished was to assemble a big and well-paid administrative staff, transmit from San Francisco low powered broadcasts to which no one listened, and distribute packets of free seeds to Philippine farmers.

Most unofficial or semi-official activities that depart from the dominant policy of containment simply do not get anywhere. Many of them, indeed, have folded up after bureaucratic flutter and money-spending. Some do show results, but, because these results are out of line with the central policy, they are isolated episodes, anarchic and often adventurist. This was strikingly illustrated by the disclosure, in October, 1952, of the German "resistance" group which American "secret agents" had subsidized, trained and armed. The mission of the group was supposed to be resistance activity in the case of Soviet invasion. It was brought out that the group's plans began with the assassination of eighty leading and respectable members of the West German Social Democratic Party.

In the spring of 1952, an East European political leader came to see me. He is one of the chiefs of the anti-communist Resistance of his country, and since 1942 has been a liaison officer between the internal Resistance and the exiles outside. What he told me was in sum the following:

"Something must be done to avert disaster to my country. Americans are sending individuals inside on quick 'one-shot' assignments. Someone from —— [he named a certain organization] will approach an exile and say, 'Make a quick trip inside, get a news story for broadcast use, and we will give you a thousand dollars and a passage out of Europe.' The man goes in. His mission makes no sense, and he has no political or organizational responsibility. Because he is never going back again, he doesn't take precautions or cover his tracks. He just aims to get in and out as fast as he can. The consequence is that his trail betrays the members of our own internal organization. Sometimes, through carelessness or indifference, he exposes our people; sometimes they, knowing that he comes from outside, feel it their duty to help him and are exposed in the process. Afterwards the police use the obvious traces of his visit as an excuse for repressions."

He went on: "You cannot conduct Resistance operations in this cloak-and-dagger adventurist manner. The building of a serious Resistance movement in my country or in any Soviet held nation requires two things. First there must be a firm policy commitment by your government. Your government must find ways to make it plainly known to the people inside that the United States does not accept the present arrangements as final but stands unambiguously for the liberation of the subject nations of the Soviet Empire. The captive people as a whole, the nation, must feel certain that sooner or later they will be free. All the people, the nation itself, not isolated individuals, must be made the social base of the Resistance. Second, the Resistance activities, so far as they are possible at each given stage, cannot be carried out as private adventures or commercial purchases. They must be politically and organizationally coordinated by a responsible center which includes representatives both of your government and of the captive nation in question."

4

In testimony before the Senate Subcommittee on Internal Security, Professor David N. Rowe of Yale University mentioned the following incident: "I called for a sophisticated, important, and formidable program of political warfare . . . When I put this up to Mr. [George] Kennan . . '. Kennan said, 'That is impossible. We can't do that kind of thing; we don't have people with the kind of know-how to conduct sophisticated political warfare.' " *

The reply from the formulator of the policy of containment is revealing. If Kennan's remark is interpreted to mean that "people with the kind of know-how to conduct sophisticated political warfare" have not been working for the United States government, I believe his statement to be accurate—though not quite for the reasons which Kennan would doubtless give.

Competence in anti-communist poltical warfare comprises two quite different factors. One of these is technical: specific abilities at one or more of a wide range of activities, from coining slogans or guerilla fighting to electronics and explosives. The second is a sufficient knowledge and profound rejection of communism. Competence of this double sort has neither existed in Washington nor been sought. Insofar as Washington has been fighting the Soviet-based world communist enterprise, it has been trying to do so without anti-communists.

Within the United States or in friendly nations (including the exile sections of the captive nations) there are many persons who have the required technical skills. Not

* *Hearings* on the Institute of Pacific Relations, p. 3990.

CONTAINMENT *OR* LIBERATION?

many of them work for the relevant agencies of the United States government, particularly at the higher levels. The divisions of the State Department, Central Intelligence Agency, Psychological Strategy Board, Mutual Security Agency, and other offices supposedly carrying on political warfare are staffed for the most part by routine bureaucrats, or by persons arbitrarily transferred from unrelated tasks. Those who are recruited from civilian life, though sometimes able enough in their own right, are seldom trained technicians in fields related to political warfare. They are usually stock brokers, academic social scientists, lawyers, investment bankers, members of café or conventional society out for a fling at secret missions and Washington salons, or unattached "administrators."

Even the highest technical ability is not enough for effective anti-communist political warfare. The failures in recruiting and training able technicians are secondary, and not too difficult to overcome. The essential lack in Washington has been of knowledge and passion: lack of a thorough understanding of communism and of an unwavering commitment to fight against it; lack even of a realization that such understanding and commitment are necessary.

Men and women with this knowledge and commitment exist in the United States, in the other noncommunist countries, and among the exiles from the Soviet Empire. Few are in Washington, or working for or with the agencies of the United States government.

Within those agencies the work of which bears most directly on political warfare, no important "policy level" job has been held by a hard and informed anti-communist. Within the ranks and at working posts abroad there has been a certain number, but none in positions of influence or authority. I do not mean that the important jobs are in the hands of pro-communists (though some are). I am asserting the negative: that they are not in the hands of individuals who are both reasonably informed about communism and irrevocably committed to the struggle against it.

How are we to explain this seeming paradox, the fact that so few anti-communists are to be found in the head-quarters of the world struggle against communism? The answer lies partly in the American character, partly in a temporary cultural lag, the carry-over of attitudes and ideas developed in an earlier period to a time when they are no longer appropriate.

The circumstances of American history have promoted the strong anti-ideological tendency so marked in most Americans. The American aim is *to do a job,* and the man who has done a job becomes the admired man. Doing the job is not surrounded by theory and moralizing. In government, as in American life generally, the typical American is the "pragmatic" man.

Though not impossible, it is difficult for a person who has no feeling for ideology to comprehend an enterprise like communism. He tries to make it fit under some "prac-

203

CONTAINMENT *OR* LIBERATION?

tical" category with which he is familiar—"political party" or "gang" or "aggressor nation." Because communism has in reality nothing in common with what the practical man understands by party, gang or nation, he remains *ignorant*. But he is unaware that he is ignorant, and impatient with anyone who suggests that he must learn more if he is to conduct an effective struggle against communism and the Soviet power.

Along with the non-ideological majority there has also been, in the United States government, especially in the agencies with some relation to foreign affairs, an ideologized minority. The fact that the majority is not ideologized has given this minority an influence much in excess of its relative numbers. It has set the prevailing tone of the State Department and the various Intelligence agencies.

The leading carriers of this ideology are men who were born between 1900 and 1914—the generation and in many cases the one-time colleagues of Alger Hiss. The ideas and attitudes of these men were shaped in the context of the economic depression of the '30's and the political struggle against Hitler and Nazism. The depression left them disillusioned with traditional American capitalism. "Anti-fascism" became the core of their political being, a passion as well as an intellectual attitude. In part, their anti-fascism was a native product of "liberalism" (in the American populist sense) modified by the influence of Marx-touched writers like Vernon Parrington, John Dewey and the early Charles Beard. In part, though most

204

of them did not realize this, the specific content of their anti-fascism was moulded by communist pressures. Disguised and skillfully guided by the Popular Front strategy, these worked on them through a hundred channels—the magazines they read, the plays and movies they saw, books they discussed, organizations they joined, conferences they attended, and sometimes the man in the next office or at the next seat around the dinner table.

Their vision of the contemporary world and the forces active within it was subtly distorted—concerning the causes of fascism, the nature of colonialism, the history of the Russian revolution, the laws of economic life, the meaning of art and religion, the process of education, and so much else. At the same time, deep feelings were stirred within them, and attitudes fixed so firmly that it demands an extreme crisis to undo them. Only a few of them became outright communists or Soviet agents—though in that atmosphere those few could accomplish much. But many of them were brought to believe that the communists were *allies*—allies, and even leaders, in the common fight against what was worst, against Hitler and Nazism. Communism was not like fascism, not wholly evil as fascism was, because—they were taught without knowing that they were being taught—communism "has the same ideals that we have, even if we differ on methods." And their political passion, their hatred, was concentrated and directed against Nazism. Other political things—nations or Churches or even communism—they might intellectually disagree with and practically reject. It was only about Nazism that they *felt* strongly.

This complex of ideas and attitudes prevailed, appropriately enough, through the period of war in alliance with Stalin against Hitler. Suddenly, in 1946, the men formed in that ideological pattern, occupying the key posts of government, were confronted through a sharp turn of history's wheel by a task never written in their philosophy. Now they were called on to be leaders in the fight against their former associates, the communists, and against "the great Soviet experiment." Small wonder that there have been dismay, stumbling and confusion! Small wonder that hard anti-communists are not welcome at their side—for they were taught to regard all hard anti-communists as "fascists at heart."

The Washington atmosphere of these recent years was perfectly expressed by the highest foreign policy officer, the Secretary of State, Dean Acheson, when he declined to turn his back on a Soviet agent.* This act was not isolated but typical. Acheson's friends and associates, the members of his former law firm (to which he returns whenever he is out of a government job),** collected thousands of dollars for the Hiss defense funds, and still number Alger Hiss' brother Donald, accused by the same witness of the same acts, among their partners. At Wash-

---

* There would have been nothing to comment on if Acheson had been acting merely as an individual in relation to an individual friend, Alger Hiss. So to act, he would, of course, have had to resign as Secretary of State.

** Covington & Burling.

ington dinners and cocktail parties held or attended by State Department and Intelligence officials, no bitterness or contempt was ever expressed against Alger Hiss. At those same gatherings no vile and shameless slander against Whittaker Chambers was omitted.

At a small dinner party long after the end of the first Hiss trial, I heard Charles Bohlen, ranked along with George Kennan as the leading State Department expert on affairs Soviet and communist, state his lack of conviction that Hiss was guilty. A year and a half later I listened one evening in Alexandria to Mr. and Mrs. De Forest Van Slyck as they ardently defended the political integrity of Owen Lattimore, and even more ardently denounced Lattimore's critics. This would have been a forgivable mistake in an average citizen, but Van Slyck was (and I presume still is) an important officer of the nation's highest intelligence body, the Central Intelligence Agency. A year later, in 1952, after ten months of the Internal Security Subcommittee investigation which led to the conclusion that Lattimore was from the 1930's "a conscious articulate instrument of the Soviet conspiracy," I heard Van Slyck's still more influential C. I. A. colleague, Professor Sherman Kent, and Mrs. Kent, continue to doubt that anything could be politically wrong with so distinguished a scholar as Owen Lattimore.*

* It is not necessary to agree fully with Senator McCarthy's or the Subcommittee's characterizations of Lattimore in order to be convinced that Lattimore's influence on American policy and opinion has turned out more happily for Moscow than for Americans.

In estimating basic attitudes, psychology suggests as the most accurate rule: By their emotions shall ye know them. Whom does a man hate, whom does he love, at what is he bitter, toward whom tolerant? Although George Kennan is unquestionably anti-Soviet and from a rational standpoint anti-communist, nowhere in his published writings does one ever find expressed in the texture of his style a powerful emotion concerning communism, a hatred of communism. The analysis and rejection, which are there, are always pale and abstract. Yet Kennan does express emotion in his writing, sometimes strongly. This emotion is invariably directed against the same target— the "politicians, commentators, and publicity-seekers of all sorts . . ." who offer "counsels of impatience and hatred" in place of the "counsels of moderation . . . deluging in noise and filth anyone who gets in their way . . . fanning . . . mass emotions and . . . sowing . . . bitterness, suspicion, and intolerance:" * in less fancy words, the anti-communist critics of the Acheson regime in the State Department.

In the Acheson climate the winds were predictable. It could always be foretold that they would blow cold and stormy against Senators McCarthy and McCarran, against any "friendly" witness who aided the Internal Security Subcommittee's steady probing into the communist and pro-communist infiltration of American life, against the ex-communists who gave direct and sorrowful testimony

* *American Diplomacy, 1900-50;* p. 62.

to the working of the world conspiracy. Equally certain were the soft breezes of excuse, "explanation," tolerant defense or easy denial for a William Remington (convicted of perjury for denying that he was a communist, and up for retrial on a technicality) or a John Stewart Service (indicted in the *Amerasia* theft of classified government documents and finally in 1952 dismissed from the State Department by order of the Civil Service Loyalty Review Board).

John P. Davies, Jr., a permanent official at the highest level of the Foreign Service, long active in the Far Eastern division of the State Department, and for several years a leading member of the Policy Planning staff, was assigned in 1952 to a high policy function in Germany. Early in 1952 Lyle H. Munson gave sworn and documented testimony concerning John P. Davies to the Internal Security Subcommittee. Munson swore that in November 1949, when he was an employee of the Central Intelligence Agency, he and a colleague had an official interview with Davies. Davies, Munson stated under oath, urged that the Central Intelligence Agency should set up a special "covert" unit to "consult and guide OPC [a branch of C. I. A.] in certain activities affecting the Far East." Davies proposed as the persons to constitute this unit: Benjamin K. Schwartz, Edgar Snow, Agnes Smedley, Anna Louise Strong, Professor John K. Fairbank and Mrs. Fairbank. It is now known that Agnes Smedley was a Soviet agent, a member of the Sorge espionage network.

Anna Louise Strong has been a communist for decades, and a prominent pro-Soviet journalist and editor. Fairbank has been identified in sworn testimony as a communist (though he denies it), and Edgar Snow became popular as a writer through articles favorable to the Chinese communists.

Munson's testimony was flatly denied under oath by Davies. It has been fully corroborated under oath by the colleague who was with Munson at the interview. In spite of the Senate Judiciary Committee's request and demand, the Department of Justice did nothing, at any rate prior to Election Day 1952, toward submitting to a Grand Jury "the question of whether perjury has been committed . . . by John P. Davies, Jr." As for the State Department and the Central Intelligence Agency, they have tried to suffocate this amazing incident under rules of secrecy which have no objective justification, inasmuch as national security can be affected only favorably by the fullest disclosure.

The State Department, following Munson's testimony, declared publicly that it had made a "complete investigation" of the affair, and found that there was nothing to it. Some skepticism about the completeness of this investigation is perhaps called for by the fact that it did not question either Munson or his colleague—the only two human beings besides Davies who were present at the original incident. Meanwhile, though not publicly, the State Department and its political subordinates in the

Central Intelligence Agency acted more vigorously on other fronts: to protect Davies and advance his career; and to get rid of Munson and others who, having knowledge of the matter (which was rather widespread), had shown too strong an aversion for Davies' modest proposal.

The American foreign policy of the anti-Nazi epoch, which has carried over into the early years of the anti-communist age, has another characteristic that bears on the possibility of effective political warfare. The policy has been conducted without *honor*. There are some who say that honor in politics went out with feudalism, and breathed its last when faithless Louis XI beat the chivalric Charles of Burgundy. Surely there has been a post-Renaissance honor that lasted, if with deviations, well into the 19th century, and has not yet wholly disappeared from the world. The recent directors of American foreign policy, however, do not seem to recognize any claims of *honor*.

Consider, for example, American relations with France from 1940-47. Who was one's friend, ally, colleague? Pétain for a while, according to all official behavior. Then Giraud. Then Giraud ditched for Darlan. Then Darlan renounced *in memoriam,* and De Gaulle "used" for his influence on the growing Resistance and as a symbol of the French nation. And then, after he had "served his purpose," the stubbornly unservile De Gaulle thrown aside for the more flexible-kneed socialists and centrists of the post-war "Third Force." Or think of Draja Mihailovitch, the first in Yugoslavia to fight for freedom and the West, against both forms of totalitarianism. American money and arms were diverted to the communist terrorist, Tito, to help him subvert, defame and murder Mihailovitch. And Chiang Kai-shek, who, longer than any other of the world's leaders, has held out against communist imperialism, and who resisted as America's ally every blow and every blandishment of Japanese imperialism, smeared with lies and filth in the State Department's official White Paper.

What of Angus Ward, stalwart member of the government's own Foreign Service, who after rotting a year in Chinese communist custody was banished by Acheson to Africa? or William Oatis, permitted without reprisal to be framed and jailed by Czech communists, and left to grow old in prison while Czech diplomats continue to be received at the White House? or the thousands—literally thousands—of other Americans in communist jails and slave camps? What of the dozens of Berlin anti-communists who, kidnapped by Soviet agents from their homes in the United States sector, vanish forever into the torture cells of the communist zone? What of General Anders, who formed and led the Polish Third Army out of the depths of Russia, through the Middle East, to the slopes of Monte Cassino and the Gothic line? and General Bor-Komorowski, the leader of the incredible Warsaw rising deliberately sabotaged by the Red Army at the city gates?

These Poles are outcasts, while the leaders of the United States government drink and eat and confer with Moscow's Polish stooges.

Would it not have been found unseemly by our grandfathers that American leaders should negotiate, discuss—and shake hands with the same men who at their next breath defile the air with their tales of "American germ warfare" and "medical experiments"?

Machiavelli insisted that "states are not run by prayerbooks," and I do not wish to pretend that a modern government in the complex modern world can act like a Don Quixote on the bright field of honor. But honor still has a place in the relations among human beings. You can buy agents, but not friends or allies or comrades; and when you buy you always risk being outbid. If the United States is to succeed in political warfare against Soviet communism, it must have friends who are firm under all circumstances, even the blackest, who are ready to go through to the end. Surely a man of honor is most likely to find such friends. If we do not ourselves honor our own words, who will honor them?

I conclude this inquiry into the question whether the United States can conduct effective anti-communist political warfare with doubt. The human and material resources are available, or can be found and trained. It is not clear whether the nation possesses the necessary temperament, insight and will. Of one conclusion we may be certain: political warfare, dynamically carried out and vast in scale, is the only alternative to unlimited nuclear war.

Part Three

LIBERATION

CHAPTER TEN

The Policy of Liberation

FOR THE UNITED STATES, foreign policy means policy toward world communism and the Soviet Union. The range of choice is restricted to three possibilities: appeasement, containment, liberation. Other and more elaborate names may be used, but when we strip off the wrapping, we shall find one of just these three.

Besides these three, what policy could there even conceivably be? They empty the barrel. Your purpose can be to stand off the Soviet Empire by firmly bottling it up within its present boundaries (whatever these happen to be at the given moment). That is: *containment.* You can accept communism as a legitimate child of human civilization, and therefore wish to bring the Soviet Empire within the family of nations. Because the Soviet imperial state is a totalitarian power which seeks world domination, this is equivalent to accepting the extension of Soviet control. In a word: *appeasement.* You can aim to get rid of Soviet rule, or at least reduce it to a scale which would no longer threaten all mankind. That is: *liberation.*

You must either hold Soviet power where it is or let it advance or thrust it back.

It can be argued that the three alternatives reduce to two. Though logically conceivable, we have found by analysis and experience that the policy of containment is historically impossible. At most, containment can be a temporary expedient, a transition. As the transition is completed, containment must move toward one or the other of the two major poles, toward appeasement or liberation.

I am inclined to think that the defenders of containment have sensed the historical vacuum upon which their position has rested. The containment period has brought into a kind of united front two groups with contrary perspectives which for a few years happened to intersect. One, partly out of ignorance, partly out of softness toward communism, believes at heart in appeasement. This group regards containment as a maneuver designed, on the one hand, to reach a better spot from which to negotiate with Moscow, and on the other, to quiet the more extreme anti-Soviet feelings at home, which might explode in the face of an open policy of appeasement. I should place in this appeasement wing Dean Acheson and many of those who were closely associated with him in the Department of State.

At the same time, others who went along with the policy of containment, including many among the military and not a few in the less prominent offices of the Department of State itself, looked on containment as a maneuver with a very different motivation. This second group has been by conviction or temperament for liberation, even if the name was not much used. It felt that so positive and sharp a policy as liberation could not be reached in a single jump from the friendly appeasement of war time and the post-war demobilization. There had to be an intermission during which the nation could reverse the demobilization process, get rid of the ideological hangover from the good-old-Joe days, and encourage its allies. Containment, valueless for its own sake, was necessary as a bridge to the firm shore of liberation.

What exactly is meant by a policy of liberation? Let me begin an answer by quoting the statement of a Hungarian exile, Francis Honti:

"As is usually the case with emigrés, the political exiles from Central and Eastern Europe are divided upon many issues, but whatever may be our beliefs we neverthless pursue the same object, that is the liberation of our countries from Soviet domination. The primary condition for such liberation must be to end the Russian occupation, whether direct or indirect. The first form of occupation consists in maintaining on our territories armed forces, professional soldiers and Russian police, while the second is more or less camouflaged though no less oppressive, being carried out through communist agents and organizations imposed by Moscow and working for her benefit.

But liberation will not be effective if we expel only the Russians and their stooges. Since 1945 we have had every reason for not identifying the defeat and departure of the occupants with true liberation, and we have learned from most painful experience that a country is effectively liberated only if it regains its independence. Liberation for us, and for all peoples who wish to live in dignity and enjoy equality of rights, must consist in the restoration of national independence." *

To this statement it is necessary to make two immediate additions. Mr. Honti seems to interpret "liberation" as if "national liberation" were alone in question. In political weight national liberation is primary, but the policy seeks individual and social liberation as well. Communist imperialism enslaves individuals, classes, religions and other social groups. The goal of liberation therefore includes freeing the subjects of the Soviet Empire as individuals, as workers, as worshippers, as members of families. If the Soviet subjects achieve liberation, this will mean not only that they have won national freedom but that they will be free from slave camps and the secret police, free to worship God as they see fit, free (if they so choose) to own and cultivate their own land and to work with their own tools, free to make peace with their fellow-men.

Second, liberation applies to the whole Soviet Empire, and is not limited to the regions which were seized at the end of the second World War and thereafter. Morally,

* *The Eastern Quarterly,* Vol. V, No. 3/4, August-October, 1952.

such a restriction is indefensible. Practically, to make it would promote an irreconcilable hostility between the inhabitants of the original Soviet Union and those of the newly captive nations.

There is thus nothing mysterious about the policy of liberation. Its goal is freedom for the peoples and nations now enslaved by the Russian-centered Soviet state system —freedom for all the peoples and nations now under communist domination, including the Russian people. For the United States to adopt the policy of liberation will mean in the first instance simply that a responsible decision by the government commits the country to that goal. The basic commitment must be open: we have seen in the preceding chapter that it is impossible to have a "secret" policy of liberation. There is no need at the beginning for an official statement of just how the goal will be reached, nor would it be proper at any time for Americans to try to prescribe in detail the political and social arrangements that will replace the Soviet state system.

2

Among those who accept the goal of liberation there will inevitably be disputes over means and methods. However sharp, these will be less deep and more productive than the dispute over general policy, the intensity of which has been increasing since the latter part of 1949—

the date when the Soviet atomic explosion and the communist conquest of the Chinese mainland proved objectively that containment had collapsed.

The policy of liberation will affect all fields of national endeavor—diplomatic, economic, psychological, military. Liberation cannot be a Sunday doctrine, but must inform and guide day by day, routine behavior, as well as the great and special actions. So it has been with containment.

The containment principle is to try to hold the line, but never to aim beyond it. Therefore, under containment, the Korean armistice boundary had to be the 38th parallel; Chinese Nationalist units from Formosa cannot be permitted to operate on the mainland; the American spokesmen in the United Nations must repudiate the terms of a law passed by Congress to arm exile military units; the anti-communist majority of the Albanian populace cannot be rallied to take the rather short jump out of the Soviet Empire; American and allied negotiators must tamely submit to infamous indignities in the Korean negotiating ritual; American power must sit idly by while American citizens are "brain washed" by communist inquisitors; American spokesmen everywhere have got to "avoid provocation," yield the initiative, and stay strictly on the defensive. This is the way it has been and had to be, under the policy of containment. Conversely, this is in each case the opposite of the way it will necessarily be if the policy of liberation is translated into action.

222

Following the commitment of the United States to the objective, the next act under a policy of liberation will be the communication of the decision to the inhabitants of the Soviet Empire, and to the world at large. The Soviet subjects, and the leaders also, know that the survival of the Soviet system depends in the last analysis on the United States. If the United States acquiesces in the system's permanence, if the policy of containment (which is equivalent to acquiescence) continues or is succeeded by appeasement, then the problem is settled. The remaining opposition will wither, and talk of anti-communist Resistance will become mere provocation. A genuine Resistance can develop only out of the conviction that the present state of affairs is temporary, that the system will not endure. This conviction must be shared by the masses, not confined to exceptional and perhaps eccentric individuals. Isolated Letts and Kazakhs and Chinese will never shake the Soviet system. The policy of liberation addresses itself to entire nations and peoples: its goal is freedom, not subversion.

Words alone ("propaganda") will not be enough to convince the masses of the American commitment to liberation. This must be daily demonstrated in action. The content of the demonstration will be threefold: all-sided political warfare; auxiliary military and paramilitary actions where called for; adequate preparation for whatever military action may be required in the future. The United States is of course already busy along these three lines. The shift in policy will step up the scale and tempo, particularly of political warfare, and focus all activities both political and military on the objective of liberation.

Because I am here concerned with the basic issue of policy, I do not want to clutter up the analysis with technical problems of application. I should like merely to use a few examples to show how the perspective of liberation would be concretely expressed in political warfare actions.

The outlook of liberation implies that the peoples and nations now subject to Soviet imperial domination are allies of the United States, and not either enemies or mere agents. The adoption of the policy of liberation would demand, therefore, that so far as possible the United States treat them as allies. This means that the United States would consider authentic representatives of these nations as the spokesmen for friendly state powers. From the point of view of liberation the present communist governments are not authentic, but are illegitimate usurpers. It follows that wherever there is any plausible basis for doing so, some sort of recognition should be extended to "free" (now necessarily exile) governments or to representative national committees.

The United States, even under the policy of containment, has continued to recognize the free governments of the Baltic nations, and to refuse to give legal acceptance to the incorporation of their territories within the Soviet Empire. The perspective of liberation suggests that this recognition should be taken more seriously, and that in terms of diplomacy and material aid the officials of the free Baltic governments should be treated in the same way as those of other allied powers.

It would be entirely proper, and legally justified, to withdraw recognition from the puppet Warsaw government of Poland in favor of the Free Polish ("London") government, which has been continuously recognized by a number of countries, including Spain, Lebanon, Portugal, and several South American nations. It goes without saying that under the policy of liberation any idea of recognizing the Chinese communist government would be dropped.

The exact form of relations with the exile representatives of other captive countries would have to be worked out in terms of the specific situation in each case. It is desirable to preserve a maximum of flexibility, and to realize that the function of exile groups is always transitional. In the end, the political outcome rests on those who remain, not on the exiles. At the same time, the United States should keep searching for forms which express the conviction of ultimate freedom, should always act *as if* the present captivity were only an episode and liberation inevitable.

A nation does not fully exist unless it can defend itself: that is, unless it has an army. Under the policy of liberation, therefore, an immediate project would be the formation of military units under the flags of the now captive

225

nations. Whether these units ought to be put under NATO command, under the United Nations (as in the Korean command), or attached to the United States armed forces is a technical question to be answered in practical terms. The decision to bring them into existence is not technical but political, and of immense importance, above all for its potential effect within the Soviet sphere.

A nation must have trained and loyal citizens to carry on the administrative and professional work which its social existence requires. Since these are being weeded out, corrupted or destroyed by the communist regimes at home, at least some individuals—cadres, one might say— must be assembled abroad. This means that institutions such as the modest Free Europe University in Exile should be developed on a large scale, and that the political shackles should be removed from them, so that they will be quite openly preparing men and women to take up the civic responsibilities of their liberated homelands.

These activities—political, economic, military, educational—necessarily originate for the time being in the non-communist world. In all cases, their focus and objective are inside the Soviet sphere. Geopolitically, they are applications of what I have called the East European strategy. It is to be assumed that simultaneously with them the effort will be made to establish liaison with the homelands: through every media of communication and, where possible, directly by courier and in person. These various activities, based as they are on the assumption of

THE POLICY OF LIBERATION

the inevitabilty of liberation, will themselves provide much of the content of communication. What could more enhearten the subject peoples or more dismay their rulers than news of a representative of free Poland sitting in the councils of NATO; free regiments marching under the flags of Rumania, Esthonia, Russia; a free Ukrainian unit capturing a hill in Korea or wiping out one of Ho Chi Minh's detachments in Indochina; a class of a thousand young East Europeans graduating from their free University with degrees in administration, agriculture and engineering; twenty thousand East European, Chinese and Russian exiles combining military training with agriculture in North Africa; a NATO destroyer manned by Baltic seamen; free spokesmen of all the captive nations received with honor in Whitehall, the Quai d'Orsay and the Department of State?

A program of liberation will at once transform the problem of escapees, who have been sitting like undigestible dough on the stomach of the free world. There will be more than enough for escapees to do, in fields calling for a variety of mental, moral and physical qualifications. It will become possible to organize a deliberate campaign of escapes, designed to weaken the enemy at critical points, and to fill gaps in our own forces.

The goal of the policy of liberation is to free men from the totalitarian tyranny of communism. Communist power, and therefore anti-communist political warfare, operates outside as well as within the Soviet sphere. The liberation perspective suggests that the principal strategic aim in the non-Soviet nations should be the *outlawing* of the communist enterprise. I use this word in a double sense, meaning: to convince public opinion of the fact that communism is an intellectual and moral "outlaw"—outside of the permissible boundaries of the civilized community; and, second, to draw the practical conclusion from this by illegalizing and suppressing the organized communist movement. This strategic aim is implicit in the policy of liberation, both because it is part of the task of freeing men from the communist conspiracy and also because no nation can stand firm against Soviet pressure, much less fight the Red Army, if it is bled internally by large-scale communist activity.

3

The policy of liberation recognizes the right to self-determination and therefore to independence of all the nations of the Soviet Empire, including the nations located within the pre-1939 Soviet boundaries. If liberation actually leads to the fractionalizing of the present Soviet Empire into several dozen wholly independent sovereign and rival states, this will at least remove the intolerable threat to world security which exists because of the control of all central Eurasia by a single aggressive power apparatus. Even such a super-Balkanization would thus be preferable to the present state of affairs, but it would

228

not be occasion for unmixed rejoicing. It would make impossible the efficient economic organization of Central and Eastern Europe. It would keep that area in a permanent state of political instability, with a myriad petty rivalries and conflicts almost certainly leading to war and near-war. In all probability, the independence of the newly freed nations would not last long.

These consequences can be avoided by the voluntary unification, to one or another degree and in one or another form, of Central and Eastern Europe. Far from being contrary to the perspective of liberation, an East European Federation, itself doubtless part of a Federated Europe, is a necessary support of liberation. Liberation, independence, federation: the three are links in the same policy chain.

In the article from which I have already quoted, the Hungarian, Francis Honti, correctly observes:

The essential condition of our true and lasting liberation . . . consists in this indispensable and permanent unity of our nations. Isolated we are a mosaic of states and nations, an easy prey; united we form a compact body of 150 million men, with great economic prospects and considerable military potential, able to resist any attempts at domination, either Russian or German. Instead of being a subject of constant worry to the world our region would become a factor of political stability. By our common efforts . . . we could considerably raise the standard of living of the population. Germany and Russia would also profit by this, for the slavery and misfortune of her neighbors are not the real conditions for the prosperity and happiness of any nation. The unity of our countries would be a guarantee of peace not only for ourselves but also for our neighbors . . .*

It would be impossible and improper for the United States government to decide just what peoples and nations would be included within an East European Federation, just how it would be internally organized, and how related to western Europe. But to favor the Federation principle, and to further it in action, is an essential element of the policy of liberation. Just as propaganda, organization, clandestine operations and all other political warfare activities should proceed *as if* liberation were certain, so should they assume the future federation of the liberated nations. In promoting federation the United States should not hesitate to run, if necessary, counter to the jealousies and ambitions of some of the East Europeans themselves or the preferences of German and Russian chauvinists who may want to keep a soft pillow to punch.

* *Ibid.*, p. 5. Mr. Honti assumes in stating the population as 150 million that Ukraine and Byelorussia will be part of the unified East European political structure.

4

The policy of liberation unavoidably confronts a special problem which is delicate, difficult, and, for Americans, unfamiliar. This problem, to which I have already referred, is sometimes called "the Soviet nationalities question." Let us review its origin.

The pre-1939 Soviet Union was not a single nation, but a system of nations in which Russia held a dominant and therefore imperial relation toward the rest. At the same time the Russian people were themselves oppressed by the communist regime. Though the Russians are the largest national group within the Soviet Union, they are admittedly a minority of the total population. Exact figures are not available, but out of a Soviet population of roughly 200 million there are about 90 million Russians.

The remaining 110 million are divided into many score nations and ethnic groups. Among the chief of these are: the Ukrainians, with 35-40 million; the Moslem Turkish groups which total in all about 25 million; Byelorussia, with 10 million; various non-Russian Cossack groups, about 10 million; Georgia, more than 3 million; Azerbaijan, about 3 million. Most of these non-Russian nations were conquered by Russia (Muscovy) only in comparatively recent times, and they have never been entirely pacified. They have shared in the world-wide upsurge of national sentiment which has gone on for a hundred and fifty years, and which in the latest period has brought independent existence to India, Indonesia, Eire, Burma and the Philippines and has given birth even to such unexpected nations as Israel and Pakistan.

At the end of the first World War, the major non-Russian nations declared their independence, and fought to keep it until, conquered by the Red Army, they were brought back under the control of a now-communist Moscow. The three Baltic nations, also now numbered by Moscow among the constituent Soviet republics, preserved independence until 1940.

In 1941, when the Reichswehr invaded the Soviet Union, the non-Russian nations again tried to take advantage of the turmoil of war to break away from Moscow. Non-Russian soldiers surrendered by hundreds of thousands, until Nazi behavior, based upon the conception that all east Europeans are subhuman, gradually showed most of them, as it also did those Russians who had surrendered in the hope of escaping communism, that freedom could not be found through Hitler.

Most Americans and west Europeans use the term "Russian" to refer indiscriminately to any inhabitant of the Soviet Union. Within the Soviet Union, "Russian" means only an ethnic Russian, and the term would not be applied to a Georgian, Chechen, Ukrainian, Kazakh, Uzbek or any of the others. The largest of the non-Russian nations give their names to "republics" of the "Union of Socialist Soviet Republics." There is, of course, no "Soviet language." Each of the nations has its own literature, language, costumes and traditions.

Recognizing the political energy potential of the non-Russian nations, the Kremlin plans its course toward them with great care, and mingles cycles of terror and brutal Russification with interludes of shrewd appeasement and flattery. Not once but several times the entire leading strata of the non-Russian republics have been purged. Campaigns against Ukrainian, Georgian, Armenian or whichever "reactionary chauvinism" are routine performances.

On the other tack, Moscow poses as the preserver of the culture of the non-Russian nations. Though the substance of power is never shared, the lesser nations are granted some of the trappings. Particularly striking was the creation of "foreign offices" for Ukraine and Byelorussia, and Moscow's insistence—successfully put at Yalta—that both should be given representation in the United Nations. Most commentators explained this by saying that Moscow wanted more votes in the Assembly. That may have been a minor reason—though Moscow has always known that a few votes more or less are of no real importance. The principal motive was undoubtedly to try to give a safe and diverting outlet to the pressure of Ukrainian and Byelorussian nationalism.

For a program of liberation, the Soviet "nationalities question" comes down to this: does the perspective of liberation, independence, and voluntary federation apply only to the nations brought under Soviet rule subsequent to 1939 (the "satellites"), or does it apply also to the nations included within the pre-1939 Soviet Union? On this issue there is bitter conflict among the exile groups. Most of the Russian exile organizations hold that Russians and non-Russians are oppressed equally by communism, and that liberation should mean the freeing of all the inhabitants of the Soviet Union, taken collectively, from the communist tyranny. They say that a program which stresses self-determination and possible independence for the non-Russian nations is "separatism," that the Russian people regard it as "dismemberment" of "their country," and that its effect would be to make the Russians rally around the communists as the only defenders of the integrity of the fatherland.

Nearly all non-Russian exile groups, including those from the newly captive countries, reject these Russian arguments. They insist that the non-Russian Soviet nations are doubly oppressed, with communist tyranny added to a Russian imperialism which goes back long before the communist revolution and has continued without interruption thereafter. In fact, many of them argue that communism is simply the latest form of Russian imperialism. Liberation must mean the full right of self-determination for the non-Russian nations, including their right to independence and to a settlement of their future relation to Russia as they see fit.

Most of the non-Russians take for granted that nations

THE POLICY OF LIBERATION

like Ukraine, Byelorussia and Georgia will seek federation and unity to their west, not with Russia. They say that the non-Russian peoples can be stirred to effective resistance only by the unambiguous perspective of national and social freedom, and that after the hard lessons of a long history the masses have little interest in a mere turn from one to another form of Russian domination. They claim, finally, that this unmixed prospect of liberation is in no way counter to the will and interest of the Russian people, who having always themselves suffered under the heel of their own imperialist governing class, can only benefit by the change of the Russian state from an imperialist oppressor to a friendly and peaceful neighbor.

Extremists among the Russian exiles tend toward a neo-Russian (non-communist) imperialism, and the extremists of the other side toward a crude anti-Russianism. Both extremes are surely to be avoided, and there is no reason for Americans to plan in full the political reconstruction of Soviet territory following the breakdown of the Soviet regime—a procedure which would be useless as well as absurd. At the same time, some sort of answer to the key problem of principle has got to be given. It affects the day by day activities of political warfare as well as major preparations for the future.

If we accept the logic of the policy of liberation, we must interpret its goal as applying not only to the post-1939 captives but to all of the constituent nations of the Soviet Union, the non-Russian nations and also Russia.

235

Our proposal must be for the freedom of *all* the nations: a Ukrainian has the same right to freedom as a Pole or a Russian. Only this universal interpretation, which is recommended alike by expediency and justice, will release the centrifugal energy of all the peoples of the Soviet Empire, a power which if given a chance to express itself can shatter the imperial structure. It would be ludicrous to interpret the struggle against communism as a fight to preserve the Russian Empire. If Russians who claim to be anti-communists refuse to extend the goal of freedom to non-Russians, then we must wonder whose side such Russians will be on when a showdown comes.

It may be that exile Russians are right when they say that most Ukrainians, Georgians, Turkomen, and so on regard themselves as little brothers of the Russians and want to remain an integral part of a Russian state purged of communism. If so, well and good: but let us see. It may also be that the non-Russian exiles are correct in believing that their ethnic countrymen have had enough of Russians, and want to trust their political future to another set of ties: to an East European Federation, a united Europe, a Federation of Moslem Turks, and perhaps other combinations or variants. The policy of liberation assures them only that they have the right to choose. Even an abstractly unwise choice, if made with the spirit of the peoples behind it, will have more probability of bringing peace and stability to those troubled regions than a decision imposed by conquest.

5

I have repeatedly insisted that the essential element of the policy of liberation is *the commitment to a goal*. It will be wise to join clarity and firmness concerning the goal with much flexibility toward the methods used in its pursuit. History is cunning. We cannot be sure by just what steps or at what pace the communist yoke can be lifted. Must the complete overthrow of each of the existing governments within the Soviet sphere invariably take place, or can there be new "Titoist" shifts in which an existing government, if only as a transition move, itself breaks away from Moscow's control? Can the change come more or less peacefully, or must there always be mass violence? Is it conceivable that the Soviet Empire can break up, or begin to break up, without general war? Could a palace revolution some time after the death of Stalin lead to a significant modification of the Soviet system?

We should be modest in attempting to answer such questions ahead of time, and willing to change our answers at the call of new evidence. What we can decide in advance is that we will by our own actions work to strengthen those developments in every field that contribute to the goal of liberation, to the weakening of communism and the dissolution of the Soviet state system.

I have stressed the conduct of all-sided political warfare in pursuit of the goal. Is political warfare enough? Can

237

the goal be reached, or at least sufficiently approximated, without shooting and without general nuclear war?

Although only a fool or a liar would guarantee a complete reply, some partial truths may be stated. First, there will certainly be shooting, as there already and continuously has been. Those who talk about not "provoking" the Soviets are inclined to forget that in Greece, Iran, Malaya, the Philippines, Burma, India, Berlin, Indochina—and Korea—there have been hundreds of thousands of casualities in the anti-Soviet ranks. These increase to millions if we add, as we should, the victims of the purges and liquidations inside the Soviet Empire.

Whatever the policy, there will continue to be auxiliary military actions of various sorts. Some will be comparable to one or another of those which have already occurred. There may be new kinds: if, for example, the Albanians, aided by exiles and material help from abroad, decided to break away from the Soviet orbit; if Chinese Nationalist units from Formosa should be permitted to reenter the mainland; if a Titoist Polish government asked recognition and protection; or—at a later but not impossible stage—if the people of Czechslovakia, East Germany or Bulgaria rose against their communist masters, and called on the nations of the West to prohibit intervention by the Soviet Red Army.

Second, we can conclude from an understanding of the nature of communism and from a review of Soviet history that the Soviet Union is never in fact provoked. If

238

Moscow wants general war, then general war will begin. Not strength but weakness in the attitude of the enemy is the only factor that might speed its beginning. Moscow has not been ready for general war, and as I write (in the latter part of 1952) there is no indication that she will be in the near future. Those strong actions that have been taken since 1947 have not brought on general war, though some of them, as in Greece, Korea and Turkey, have been in themselves undeniably provocative.

Third, the policy of liberation would prove a stronger deterrent to general war than the policy of containment can possibly be. The policy of liberation, insofar as it has any success at all, strikes behind the Soviet front, and throws forces across the Soviet lines of communication. At the same time it arouses what are from the Soviet point of view the most disruptive internal elements. Strategically considered, it is hard to see what could give the Kremlin greater pause.

Fourth, we must understand that in the long run general war, though not inevitable, remains a probability, policy or no policy. Too much is at stake—indeed, the world is at stake—to assume that either side will accept defeat without a total effort to forestall it. The United States, together with whatever allies will join, must therefore prepare for general war. This necessity has no specific relation to the policy of liberation. Under the policy of containment the United States has been preparing for general war, and would have to do so under any conceivable policy except outright capitulation.

Policies either of containment or appeasement share a key defect. No matter what can be said for them during a period of peace or near-peace, they must be dropped on the outbreak of general war. About this there can presumably be no argument. Once general war starts, appeasement no longer has any meaning, and containment would be a direct prescription for defeat. Consequently, the basic policy structure must be overturned. This cannot be done quickly or without loss. Not only nationally but internationally, the pre-war policy will have built up established ways of thinking, acting and feeling, together with a particular estimate of the world situation, the nature of the opponent and what ought to be done. Then, with the beginning of general war, everyone will be expected to reverse himself abruptly, and to substitute a wholly new pattern of opinion and action.

No such discontinuity need interrupt the development of the policy of liberation. Exactly the same basic policy holds for conditions of peace, limited (cold) war, and general war. The outbreak of general war would in no way affect the substance of the policy, but only its tempo and the detailed mode of its application. This means that everything positive done under the policy of liberation counts, and does not have to be jettisoned at a change in the international weather. We are for the freedom of the peoples and nations of the Soviet Empire yesterday, today and tomorrow. In action, we promote the goal of their liberation by the means that are appropriate to the given stage. In peace and semi-peace we deny the permanence of the Soviet tyranny. In full scale war, our blows aim not at the conquest of territory but at the freeing of men and of nations.

It would be criminal if the policy of liberation were so directed as to arouse premature, narrow uprisings that would lead only to bloody repression and the loss of the most active Resistance leaders. At the same time we must ask ourselves: what if, in a captive nation, in a non-Russian Soviet nation or even in Russia itself, a broad mass uprising against the regime began? or what if one of the communist governments, supported by the majority of the people, declared against Moscow? And, in either case, what if help were then asked from the free world? Whatever the official policy, will the United States and its allies stand aside while the Red Army and the special troops of the MGB slaughter enough millions to wipe out the challenge not only from those who have come into the open but from any who might dream of freedom in the future? Would not passivity under such circumstances be a final proof of the inevitability of communist world victory?

To intervene even under those circumstances would not necessarily mean general war. Intervention in Greece and Korea have not brought general war, nor is there any indication that operations tomorrow on the Chinese mainland would do so. There are many forms of intervention, and many replies—including, of course, retreat. From Moscow's point of view, a mass revolt in part of her Empire, capable of spreading like fire in the dry season, is hardly a happy moment for starting general war. Indeed, it is not certain that Moscow would ever start general and unlimited war. She would do so only if she felt sure of victory. The fact that she has held back up to now proves that she has feared to lose rather than to gain by general war, and that she has felt more confident about the results of other modes of struggle. If successful anti-Soviet political warfare weakened the Soviet Union, then Moscow would be still less likely to dare the gamble on general war.

Finally, we may note that the policy of liberation throws the Soviet Empire on the defensive, and captures the initiative for the free world. The policy of liberation is by its essence offensive, just as containment and appeasement are essentially and unavoidably defensive. This contrast applies in every field, military, economic, political. In the present struggle for the world as in all conflict, the general law applies: only the offensive can win. When we call a policy "offensive," what we are really saying is simply that it aims to win.

CHAPTER ELEVEN

Liberation and National Defense

THREE OBJECTIONS to the policy of liberation deserve special notice. It can be argued that the allies of the United States would be unhappy about it; that it would involve the United States in a fanatic and utopian "crusade"; and that the liberation of the Soviet Empire, however desirable, is none of America's proper business, which is restricted to the defense of its own security.

It is a fact that many persons within the non-communist nations are uneasy about a shift to the perspective of liberation. We have noted some of the reasons for this, and have also seen how the policy of containment bolsters the attitude of neutralism. Containment, if successful, would mean a stalemate between Moscow and Washington. To the non-communist nations other than the United States, a stalemate seems to promise protection from all-out world war and at the same time, because of the balancing off of the two major powers, an easier chance for independent maneuvers.

There is another reason why the non-communist nations cling to the stalemate, incline toward neutralism and drag their feet in the job of building anti-Soviet power. They do not yet believe in the seriousness of American purpose. What is the United States up to? what is its objective? To these questions clear answers have not been given. Is the United States determined to weaken and if necessary eliminate the Soviet system? or does it really want some sort of accommodation with the Kremlin? and if the latter, at whose expense? Does the United States really plan to defend Western Europe? Southeast Asia? the Middle East? and if so, how?

Unless these questions are answered convincingly, in American behavior as well as by words, there is no motive for strenuous anti-Soviet action. Outside or inside the Soviet Empire, there will be no firm resistance without a reasonable chance of winning. If Washington hasn't made up its mind, why stick one's neck out? Better to keep both anchors down, avoid final choice, and hope that for all the thunder, the lightning somehow won't hit.

Under the procedures of containment, the United States has often subordinated its policy and its military preparations to the fears, prejudices and weakness of its presumptive allies. That is what gives such influence to the debilitating demagogy of Aneurin Bevan, Jawarhalal Nehru and some of the German socialists. The State Department has hoped that by not going too fast with allies, "not alarming" them, they would become convinced of

American "good intentions," and ready to accept a sterner course.

It doesn't work that way. The other nations are aware of their weakness. They know that on their own they are not able to meet the Soviet challenge. When they observe that Washington tempers its course at their bidding, the effect is not to conciliate them but to make them lose confidence in Washington. If I know little about horses and am broke besides, I am not going to be impressed with a man who asks me how to bet on the next race.

The first problem for the United States is to make up its own mind, to select and pursue its own objectives. In this pursuit, the United States would be wise to rely, so far as this is possible, on its own resources and on a strategy that grows naturally out of its own geopolitical situation. To depend on someone else is to be in the last analysis at his mercy. Surely Americans are not opposed to communism and the Soviet system only on condition that West Europeans and Indians and Arabs are also opposed. We are opposed even without and even against all the rest of the world, even if alone.

The leader of a coalition should be ready to welcome every ally but should depend on none. When the United States begins a real shift to the policy of liberation, there will unquestionably be complaints, alarms and perhaps denunciations from the camps of wanted allies. These must be expected and allowed for. They will be quieted not by yielding to them, but by the demonstration of the clarity, firmness, and adequacy of the policy decision which the United States will have taken. It will then be the turn of the other nations also to make up their minds—after all, why should France be firm if America is uncertain? When they do, and only then and in that way, the United States will begin to have allies. Up to now, there have in reality been clients and pensioners, not allies.

2

It is the intellectual fashion to be scornful of "crusades." Crusades, it is said, are as dangerous as they are futile. They arouse a fanatic spirit that hardens on both sides, and leads to insistence on the unconditional surrender of the enemy. The conflict becomes "a holy war." The crusaders' passions rule out any chance for negotiation and reasonable compromise. To adopt the policy of liberation, critics warn, would be to set out on a crusade. This we should with all urgency avoid, and instead, after "prudent and orderly measuring of the national interest," we should "admit the validity and legitimacy of power realities," in order "to seek their point of maximum equilibrium." *

I feel some sympathy for this distrust of crusades, especially because of the contemporary habit of turning everything from an election campaign to a vice cleanup into an ardent crusade for something or other. A crusade

* George F. Kennan, *op. cit.,* pp. 19 and 53.

should not be anything that beckons on a routine horizon. A crusade is special and rare. In all ordinary times and for all ordinary causes, prudence suggests that the crusading spirit should be allowed to slumber. But I cannot help feeling that there is a touch of Philistinism in the inordinate fear that a struggle against the infamy of communist despotism and for the freedom of 800 million enslaved human beings might become a crusade. Is this fear an expression of a lack of confidence in ourselves and in the rightness of our cause? Is it not curious that many of those same persons who today warn of the dangers of a crusade against communism were a few years ago the loudest in demanding a crusade against Nazism?

A campaign of liberation, properly carried out, will have many of the elements of a crusade, and will not succeed without them. Let us remark that we are not altogether free to accept or reject the idea of a crusade. There arise from time to time objective historical conditions that can be met only in terms of a crusade, and that make irrelevant any paler form of struggle. This occurs when circumstances place in active opposition to each other two ways of life, two conceptions of the nature and destiny of man, which are in ultimate contradiction.

To object to conceiving the struggle against communism as a crusade implies the belief that the opposition between the communist way and ours is not fundamental. If it is not, then the idea of a crusade is light-minded, immoral and in truth fanatic. We ought then to keep the conflict as cool and rational as we can, and to be ready at all times for negotiation, compromise and settlement.

The heart of this matter has always been clear to the communist leaders, who have known themselves to be separated from what they call "the bourgeois world" by an absolute chasm. They sometimes express this by saying that with the victory of communism pre-history will be concluded and history will begin. They give further witness by their insistence that the transition from "bourgeois society" to communism can be accomplished only by total revolution, never by gradual evolution. The communist enterprise proposes to replace society, God and man by a wholly new system of society, a new kind of man with a new "nature," and the new gods of material and historical Necessity. The communists realize that with their proposal there cannot be compromise or negotiation. What is there to compromise? You do not compromise with birth, or death. There are some questions which must be answered just Yes or No.

The communist stand forces us to decide, painful as is the process to liberal sensibilities, whether we really believe that our way is better than theirs. Are we ready to declare that Western civilization is superior—objectively superior—to Soviet totalitarianism? Do we as Americans proclaim that political freedom and representative government are better than political tyranny and the sovereignty of the secret police, better for all men, Poles and Chinese and Russians as well as French and

English and Americans? Our ancestors did not doubt the universality of their political ideal, nor did they hesitate to speak and act according to its light. The Declaration of Independence did not confine its truths to the three mile limit. If we do not think that our way is better than the Kremlin's, then what are we disputing? Let us apply for acceptance as another of the Federated Socialist Soviet Republics. We can be sure of the warmth of our welcome.

3

The third objection is related to the second. It is argued that liberation, though in itself good and to be wished for, is none of our business. Suffering, despotism and famine have always been rather widely distributed in the world. We are saddened that this is so, and we rejoice when these plagues are anywhere lightened or removed. But we cannot be every man's keeper. Our task is to strengthen the liberty and well-being of our own land and people. So far as international conflict goes, our problem is our own national defense. If we assign ourselves the job of global savior, we shall not only make a mess on the world scale, but will endanger the humbler domestic goals.

Let us agree that national security and defense are the proper objective of a government's general strategy, and that any action in the field of foreign affairs which injures national security is wrong. Let us further grant that no action is justified unless it contributes positively to national defense. The case for a policy of liberation will remain as strong as ever.

The security of the United States, and of all nations that are still independent, is in the gravest peril. The danger, a mortal danger, is a reality of the present, not a vague possibility of the future. Its exact nature, and the reason why it is so deadly and so immediate, are often misconstrued by Americans, and I think also by many Europeans.

Americans are likely to measure the gravity of the Soviet threat by the degree of probability that bombs are about to start falling. Europeans add in imagination Red Army tanks and cannon moving west across the North European plain. If both bombs and tanks seem far away, then the danger cannot be too severe, and there is no ground for acute alarm.

During the years since 1945 I have never believed that general open war was imminent. I have been convinced that it was possible to undertake large-scale anti-Soviet actions, including offensive and what are usually considered "provocative" actions, without any appreciable risk that general war would result. Looking back, I don't think that anyone can now think that general war would have begun if, for example, land convoys instead of an airlift had been used to break the Berlin blockade, if Nationalist Chinese troops had been encouraged to operate in South China, if the British had asserted their rights to the Abadan refinery by force, if the Greek army

250

LIBERATION AND NATIONAL DEFENSE

had pursued guerillas on to Bulgarian or Albanian territory, or if bombing raids had been carried beyond the Yalu. Because they do not understand the nature of communism, western leaders have been needlessly cautious.

Granted that contemporary history is too unsettled to permit the dating of predictions very far into the future, I continue to believe that Moscow will not deliberately start a general war in the next period. However that may be, it is still more important to realize that the peril to the United States (and to all other independent nations) does not depend exclusively or even primarily upon the probability and timing of general war.

This peril can be summed up in a single sentence. If the communists succeed in consolidating what they have *already* conquered, then their complete world victory is certain. The threat does not come only from what the communists may do, but from what they have done. We do not have to bring in speculation about Soviet "intentions." The simple terrible fact is that if things go on as they now are, if for the time being they merely stabilize, then we have already lost. That is why the policy of containment, even if 100% successful, is a formula for Soviet victory.

These statements are so extreme that before accepting them a sober reader may be inclined to increase his usual rate of discount. As a reinforcement to rhetoric, I urge an evening with an atlas, a world map (preferably a globe), and a good book on geography. A graduate course in geo-

CONTAINMENT *OR* LIBERATION?

politics is not needed in order to comprehend the results of such an evening's research. In unemotional charts and statistics, and in the meaning that leaps unblinkably to the eye from the map's surface, we shall find a convincing proof that the Soviet Empire, if it is able to consolidate within its present limits, will be certain to conquer the earth. The geographical approach will have omitted all the dynamism which communism draws from its world revolutionary element. Even with that omission, the present Soviet territorial base, if it is successfully integrated under the control of the monolithic and aggressive regime, is enough to guarantee the ultimate outcome.

What this means is that liberation is the only defense against a Soviet world victory. Americans, Frenchmen, Germans, Indians and Japanese should not imagine that liberation is charity, a gift for them to bestow at leisure on captive Poles, Chinese and Russians. Our own necks are at stake. At least a considerable breakup of the Soviet imperial system, a breakup which in practice would be equivalent to the process of liberation, is a minimum condition for our own survival.

The communist leaders know where they stand. They know that they can win if for the present they do no more than hold and develop what they have, and they also know that they will lose if a full-scale campaign of liberation is launched against them. Their present tactic is to divert the outside world away from the policy of liberation by means of political warfare and psychological terror, while they destroy what might be called the internal premises of liberation. By purges, indoctrination of the young, Russification, controlled starvation, falsification of culture and history, group shipment to slave labor camps and mass interchanges of populations, they carry out a conscious and systematic *genocide*. The aim of their genocide program is to wipe out of historical existence the diverse nations and ethnic groups, to dissolve them into the Soviet monolith. The process has been completed in the case of some of the smaller peoples, and is being pushed throughout the Empire. The Kremlin rightly calculates on the self-evident principle that if the nations do not exist then they can no longer fight for freedom.

At the same time, the communists seek to eliminate the basis for the independent existence of all other groups that might conceivably give structure to a campaign for liberation. The slave labor camps become an essential institution of the economy, and help to pulverize the working class. The collective farm is judged inadequate to bring about the dissolution of the peasantry. The communists therefore move to transform the collective farms into vast agricultural factories serviced by cities of proletarianized laborers with no special relation to the land. The goal is a managed totalitarian society populated by an undifferentiated Russo-Soviet Mass Man. With that goal achieved or approximated, the very meaning of liberation as of freedom would have vanished.

This, then, is the measure of our peril and its urgency. We are lost if our opponent so much as holds his own. There remains only a limited time during which it will continue to be possible to move against him. Americans will not even be granted much longer the desperate comfort that as a last resort there are always the bombs to turn to. If the political offensive is long delayed, it will be too late for bombs.

About the Author

JAMES BURNHAM, long known for his writings on politics and strategy, has been living and working in Washington for nearly four years, lecturing regularly during that period at the Naval War College in Newport, the Air War College at Maxwell Field, Ala., the National War College, the School for Advanced International Studies, and other similar institutions.

Since the end of the war he has traveled extensively abroad, in order to observe international developments at first hand, and to see and work with persons both official and unofficial who are active in anti-communism. His postwar travels have taken him once around the world, with major stops in India, Thailand, and Japan, and seven times to Europe—England, France, Belgium, Germany (including Berlin), Italy, Ireland and Sweden.

Mr. Burnham is a graduate of Princeton, with additional studies at Oxford, and has been since 1929 on the faculty of New York University, teaching most of the time in the Department of Philosophy.

He has written many articles and books, the latter including *The Managerial Revolution* (1941), *The Struggle for the World* (1947), and *The Coming Defeat of Communism* (1950).